GW00789888

ARBITRA⁻

Cases in Industrial Relations

ANTHONY KENNERLEY

PITMAN PUBLISHING

PITMAN PUBLISHING
128 Long Acre, London WC2E 9AN

A Division of Longman Group UK Limited

First published in 1994

© Longman Group UK Limited 1994

A CIP catalogue record for this book can be obtained from the British Library.

ISBN 0 273 60277 2

Typeset by Mathematical Composition Setters Ltd, Salisbury, Wiltshire.
Printed and bound in Great Britain by Bell & Bain Ltd, Glasgow.

*The Publishers' policy is to use paper manufactured
from sustainable forests.*

CONTENTS

FOREWORD

I welcome this book because it highlights the very valuable role which voluntary arbitration can play in resolving trade disputes and avoiding industrial conflict.

Arbitration is a well-tried and tested mechanism available to employers and trade unions finding themselves unable to settle a problem through direct negotiations. Its strength is that both parties commit themselves in advance voluntarily to accept the decision of an independent arbitrator, usually when the various stages of a procedure agreement have been exhausted without agreement being reached and when conciliation has also been attempted. It is ACAS' experience that arbitrators' awards, which are not legally binding, are invariably accepted and implemented by the parties.

Despite its long and demonstrably successful history, the process of arbitration is one aspect of industrial relations which has remained something of a closed book to all except those directly involved. The reason for this is the confidential nature of the proceedings. ACAS, in common with its predecessors, does not publish arbitrators' awards and it is very rare indeed for arbitration hearings to be open to members of the public. It is therefore not surprising that discussions at all levels about the nature of arbitration tend to concentrate on its broad strengths and weaknesses rather than the precise details of its use in practice.

Professor Kennerley has been a member of the ACAS arbitrators' panel for many years and has handled a wide variety of assignments in companies and organisations in both the private and public sectors. The cases he has selected provide a realistic cross section of the problem areas which frequently arise in industry. I am sure this book will prove useful to all those in the industrial relations sphere who wish to gain a deeper understanding of the way in which arbitration works. Apart from its use as teaching material, the case studies will be of real interest to managers, trade union officials and all those for whom employer/employee relationships provide the focus in their working lives.

One cautionary note: when using the case studies it is important to remember that arbitration is not a scientific discipline. An arbitrator's role is to reconcile the conflicting positions of two parties and, in providing them with the solution to their dispute, to take account of the fact that their relationship will continue long after the arbitrator's award has been issued.

Derek Evans
Chief Conciliation Officer
ACAS

PREFACE

This book contains a selection of industrial relations cases drawn from a wide variety of public and private sector organisations. The cases represent a cross section of the types of dispute which arise in the workplace and are typical of the problems which come before the Advisory, Conciliation and Arbitration Service (ACAS) and frequently go to arbitration.

The book is designed to help all those concerned with developing an understanding of the process of resolving industrial disputes. As such it is appropriate for use on industrial relations courses at all levels, for training negotiators and as an introduction to the type of problems that arise in the world of work.

Each case is based on fact and contains a union submission, a management submission and appropriate background material. They are suitable for class discussion, negotiating exercises and role playing for managers, officials and students. Although new legislation may be passed, the application of new law will only affect the range of solutions possible and not the problems described in the cases. In that sense these cases will not date since arguments over payments, gradings, demarcations, new methods of working and unfair dismissals will remain.

The service which ACAS provides is free, independent and voluntary. Advice is readily available in matters concerning employment to all parties in a dispute. If both sides agree a dispute may be referred to ACAS for conciliation. This is the process whereby an official from ACAS will attempt to negotiate an agreed solution through discussions with both sides. The majority of disputes referred to ACAS are solved amicably by this method of conciliation.

When the process of conciliation has been exhausted and there is still a failure to agree the matter may be referred to arbitration. In this case it is necessary to obtain the consent of both parties, conciliation must be considered and all agreed procedures within the organisation must have been exhausted. At this point terms of reference for the arbitrator are drawn up. Ideally these will identify the difference between the parties and specify precisely the questions which the arbitrator is being asked to determine. Both parties then make written submission to the arbitrator and to each other and the matter proceeds to a formal hearing.

The arbitrator is an independent person who has no connection with the dispute who is brought in to study the submissions made by the parties, conduct the hearing, consider the evidence and reach a judgment within the terms of reference. His decision and his report are then presented to the parties.

It is important to realise that the system is voluntary and that there is no legal requirement for an employer or a union to ask for arbitration or to accept the findings or the decision of the arbitrator. In practice the decisions are regarded as binding and are implemented on both sides. Many joint agreements within organisations stipulate that when internal grievance procedures have been exhausted the dispute will go to arbitration and that the findings will be accepted.

One of the key objectives of the whole process from advice through conciliation to arbitration is to provide a fair, realistic, helpful and long term solution to the problems which lie behind the current dispute. It is in this area that the experience and expertise of arbitrators can be most useful. While the terms of reference restrict a decision to the resolution of the current dispute the accompanying report gives the arbitrator scope to present recommendations and suggestions to the parties which may help resolve grievance issues more generally without recourse to formal procedures.

In using this case book tutors and instructors have a wide choice. The material is useful for an introduction to the workplace problems at one level but can also be used to examine legal issues, codes of practice and conditions of employment. In addition some cases give examples of job grading methods, job demarcations and pay and reward systems involving bonuses and allowances. At a more advanced level participants may be asked to set terms of reference, or to prepare a report to the parties with recommendations.

The cases tend to become more complex towards the end of the book raising issues of conflict with the law and wider political or social effects. They may be used to illustrate the difficulty of predicting the ramifications of changes in legislation or the consequences of setting precedents that will be seized upon elsewhere.

In general the analysis of all the cases will be enhanced by asking such questions as: who are the stakeholders and what are they trying to achieve? Is 'fairness' an issue? Are the terms of reference appropriate? Are the procedures and agreements which the company and its staff are bound by too constraining or too vague? And finally, what is your decision, can you support it and do you have any recommendations or suggestions beyond the terms of reference which will be helpful to both parties?

Anthony Kennerley
November 1993

ACKNOWLEDGEMENTS

The author is indebted to the Advisory, Conciliation and Arbitration Service for permission to make use of material gathered during his period as an arbitrator. Care has been taken to preserve the anonymity of the unions and companies involved. In particular I would like to thank Derek Evans, Chief Conciliation Officer at ACAS for his help and guidance regarding arbitration procedures and Paul Robertson of Management Learning Resources Ltd for his help and encouragement in the preparation of this book.

Part 1
INTRODUCTION

CHAPTER 1

The process of arbitration

What is arbitration? It is a method of resolving disputes between parties without recourse to the law. It is voluntary and the procedures have to be agreed by both sides beforehand. Consequently it requires the goodwill of both sides for the method to work and it also requires trust in the arbitrators who are asked to decide the issue.

The process works in the following way. Once the usual procedures for considering disputes within an organisation have been exhausted and have failed there usually remains the option of arbitration. Both sides must then agree to go to arbitration and contact a mutually acceptable and independent arbitrator. The parties must then agree what the terms of reference for the arbitrator are to be. These can be narrowly drawn around the particular issue or broad ranging with implications for the whole industry, but they must be agreed by both sides. Often the process of drawing up terms of reference itself leads to a solution and the ultimate step of going to arbitration is not needed.

Many large organisations have laid down and agreed procedures for selecting a panel drawn from both sides who decide on the terms of reference and how the arbitrator or panel of arbitrators will be chosen. But many do not and the usual outcome in these cases is a reference to ACAS (the Advisory, Conciliation and Arbitration Service), set up by the government although totally independent and therefore non-political.

Because the activities of ACAS are thorough, well respected and widely used to solve disputes they are worth describing in detail. They serve as a good model of how arbitration procedures can be conducted.

The process usually begins when an aggrieved individual, their union or perhaps the organisation approaches ACAS. The problem is discussed in broad outline and the party will be offered advice. This advice is totally confidential and through ACAS is free. It is usually in the form of outlining the individual's rights or, to employers, their obligations. These obligations and rights will certainly encompass all legal requirements but will often include advice on codes of practice within the industry, interpretation of joint agreements and even illustrations of precedents and practice elsewhere which may be relevant.

The advisee is then better able to approach direct negotiation with the other party and hopefully arrive at an agreed solution of the dispute. In the event that no resolution is achieved between the parties the matter may proceed to conciliation.

Conciliation

Conciliation involves that part of the process in which a third party, the conciliation officer, is invited to help the two who are in dispute. Both sides agree to go to conciliation and together they approach ACAS who will suggest an appropriate member of staff for the case. This conciliation is voluntary, impartial, confidential and free of charge. It also requires a high level of knowledge, tact and skill on behalf of the conciliation officer who has to listen to and interpret the dispute from the two opposing points of view.

Being privy to both sets of views and feelings puts the conciliation officer in a privileged position. From this awareness of both sides' attitudes and their respective positions the conciliation officer tries to bring about some movement towards a mutually acceptable solution. He or she is in a position to make suggestions to either side regarding any aspect of the dispute. They may use the typical negotiator's approach of saying 'If they were to agree to this then would you be willing to consider that?' The conciliation officer is the go-between since it is not necessary for the parties to meet. Consequently, a great many avenues can be explored hypothetically with no one losing face. Sensitivity combined with keeping faith with both both parties is the precise role of the conciliator. Confidences given to the conciliator must not be revealed to the other party without permission and no favourite solution must be pressed on either party. Only when there is confidence that a solution is probable will the leading personages of each side be brought together to make the final agreement with each other. But sometimes this process also fails.

Arbitration

The final part of the ACAS procedure is arbitration. This is usually suggested once the process of conciliation has been tried and no agreement has been reached. At this point it is recognised that an agreement is not going to be reached and therefore an acceptable solution may be found by arbitration. It is important to realise that arbitration is an outcome of a 'failure to agree'. This means that an independent person will make a decision that in all probability will satisfy neither party to the dispute. What the parties are agreeing to is to abide by the decision of the arbitrator. Going to arbitration is voluntary but it is not likely that either side will get all that it wants. However, if the dispute is at the 'failure to agree' stage there is little alternative. In one sense going to arbitration relieves both sides of the necessity to 'climb down' if passions have become heated and strong positions struck.

Terms of reference

Once it has been agreed to go to arbitration a particular methodology is followed. First, and most difficult, is the setting of the terms of reference. The conciliator is often of great assistance here particularly in pointing out ambiguities in the wording and the implications of the whole phrase. In unfair dismissals the objective may be reinstatement but, failing that, do the parties wish to set bounds to compensation terms? In grading or pay disputes do the parties wish to set conditions or limits in the terms of reference to protect the conditions of other groups of workers? Does the employer wish to limit any award to that particular section of workers and therefore clearly state this? Would a possible finding in a poorly drafted terms of reference cut across any of the conditions of service that bind all employees of this particular organisation, or, worse, might they infringe the law. This latter point may be of particular importance in regard to racial or sexual discrimination, or, for example, guaranteed maternity benefits. The expert knowledge of the conciliator or other experts from ACAS is of considerable benefit at this point.

Preparation for the hearing

Once the appropriate terms of reference have been agreed an independent arbitrator is chosen and submissions prepared. ACAS maintains a panel of 40 or 50 names of people who may be called upon to act as arbitrators. They are all persons with considerable knowledge of industrial relations law and experience of industry and business. This experience of the workplace is of great importance since it is often necessary to take into account the usual customs and practices of the business or industry concerned. A solution that may be appropriate in one setting could be quite damaging in another even though the problem and even the terms of reference may be the same.

This type of solution, which relies upon experience, knowledge and judgment, is one of the great differences between an arbitration and a legal approach either in a court of law or at an industrial tribunal. In a legal situation the issues are tightly drawn and a verdict is produced. The result is that one or other of the parties is guilty or not guilty of breaking the law and must then suffer the penalties.

Well written terms of reference and a skilled and experienced arbitrator can often bring about a solution that solves the immediate issue but also points the way to modifying some procedure or condition of service to the long term benefit of both parties. These helpful pointers may be contained in the arbitrator's report and may go beyond the specific terms of reference to be decided at the time.

Once the parties have jointly chosen a particular person as the arbitrator from the appropriate names put forward by ACAS, submissions are prepared by the two parties to the dispute. Here again the conciliator, if he is asked, may help both parties to prepare their submissions but then his or her role ends. The two written submissions by the two parties to the dispute stand alone as the evidence submitted to the arbitrator. The conciliator must have no contact with the arbitrator since he or she possesses intimate knowledge of each side's feelings and attitudes and has been given a number of confidences by both sides. None of this must be allowed to influence the arbitrator and therefore there is no link between them. The arbitrator is independent and must make a judgment based only on the written evidence submitted beforehand and such supplementary evidence given at the hearing in front of the other side. In order to preserve the fairness, the written submissions prepared for the arbitrator must also be sent to the other party. In other words all three parties come to the hearing identically prepared.

The hearing

The hearing takes the form of a committee meeting and not a court of law. Often the two parties are in separate rooms beforehand and the arbitrator has the opportunity to view the room set aside for the hearing. It is important that the seating is arranged around a table in such a way that the two sides are comfortably accommodated in a manner that allows them to communicate freely among themselves, face the other party and have equal access to the arbitrator. Usually this means that the arbitrator sits at the head of the table with the four or five persons of each party ranged down the sides with the lead speaker nearest to the arbitrator.

Once satisfied with the arrangements the arbitrator sends for the two parties' members to assemble in the hearing room. It is of crucial importance that the arbitrator does not spend time in the sole company of one side or the other because of the implied opportunity to be privately influenced. When everyone has assembled introductions are made and the arbitrator usually opens the proceedings with a preamble.

The preamble takes the form of enquiring if everyone is familiar with the form of an arbitration hearing or has attended one. Invariably this gives an opportunity for the arbitrator to explain that it is not a court of law and that the objective is to obtain the best and fairest solution within the terms of reference. To that end it is of benefit to all sides to be as open and forthcoming as possible since the arbitrator starts from a position of no knowledge of the case other than what he has read in the two submissions. The arbitrator may say that it is important for him to learn why members feel as they do about the current issue and to ascertain any background details which may help him to understand the situation in the workplace better.

The hearing is to be informal and the arbitrator will act as a chairman. A careful list is taken of the speakers and witnesses present and their particular job titles and roles. The arbitrator will ask if both sides have exchanged written submissions and will enquire formally of each side that they voluntarily undertake to accept the decision of the arbitrator as binding. Having established all of this in a slightly formal way the arbitrator will then ask the lead speakers to present the key points of their case. After this the hearing becomes more informal as questions by either side or the arbitrator are asked and answers challenged. Eventually the arbitrator will say that he believes he has sufficient understanding of the situation unless there are any remaining key points to be made. The hearing is then closed.

The conduct of a hearing is a delicate balance. The arbitrator must maintain control but still allow the debate to flow freely. Often a touch of humour helps to lighten an awkward moment. If an argument develops this has to be stopped at once and a new way found to elucidate the point. It is also sometimes difficult to assess whether a seemingly irrelevant discourse should be allowed to run in case it reveals some point of value or whether it should be challenged. Usually a hearing lasts two or three hours before the arbitrator closes it.

The report

After the hearing the arbitrator is left to prepare a report and make the award. He has the written submissions and his notes of the hearing to guide him together with his impressions of the various witnesses and the strength of their convictions.

The report has several parts. It begins with the minute of appointment by ACAS, goes on to give the date and location of the hearing and states the terms of reference. This is followed by a list of all the persons attending the hearing, their job titles and the roles they are filling at the hearing. These preliminary parts of the report are straightforward and factual. The substance of the report follows in five further parts. These are the background to the dispute, a precis of the two submissions, the arbitrator's comment and finally the award.

The arbitrator is free to make a very full and thorough report but usually it is only necessary to list the key elements. Apart from the award the most important part is the arbitrator's comment. Here the arbitrator may give reasons for the award, or he need not. He may also make recommendations, or more probably suggestions, which he feels may be helpful to the parties. However, there is no obligation for the arbitrator to make detailed comments or give reasons or to make recommendations. It depends on the case.

The award

When considering the award, the arbitrator must have regard to all the pertinent factors. It is particularly important to put the appropriate construction on custom and practice. Some examples may be helpful here.

When is it appropriate for a person to take a drink during working hours? For many years beer was freely available in the workplace for steelworks operating open furnaces in order for the men to replace body fluids. It is a practice that would be frowned on nowadays. But consider the situation of, say, construction workers who visit the only local provider of food at lunch-time, a public house, for a 'pie and a pint'. Is this bad practice? Another similar issue is the marketing manager who entertains a client to a good lunch with alcoholic beverages. How does the arbitrator treat the charge of being under the influence of drink?

Similarly, remarks that would pass for harmless banter among men in a shipyard would be swiftly reported as sexual harassment in a mixed office. In another situation a particular group, perhaps a new computer section, begins to exhibit coercive behaviours that are viewed by others as intellectual put-downs. What influence have all these factors on the way in which the arbitrator fashions the award? Ultimately it is a personal assessment and a judgment is made within the terms of reference. The case is closed and the report and award are sent by ACAS to both parties in a manner which ensures that they are both informed at the same time.

CHAPTER 2

Use of the case studies

The nine case studies presented in this book have been carefully selected to give a wide representation of the types of problem which arise in industrial relations. Students who have little or no knowledge of working life will have difficulty in relating to many of the cases and will lack understanding of such important factors as the cultural norms on the factory floor or in the design office. Those who have experience tend to take sides and it is the task of the tutor or facilitator to present the counter-points if matters become cut and dried one way or the other.

There is an increasing complexity towards the end of the book and wider issues begin to enter. The assessment of managerial responsibilities, the definition of bonus and the setting of a pay increase by comparison with large national companies are all issues for debate in their own right. The range of problems includes job grading, the introduction of new procedures and equipment, productivity schemes, job demarcations and unfair dismissal. The selection is designed to cover most aspects of an industrial relations course.

In each case study there are papers giving both the employer's and the union's side of the dispute. In addition there are associated documents which are common to both sides. These are of great value in introducing the various forms of structures in agreements between management and unions and serve as a window into industrial practice.

Course participants of all ages and experience benefit greatly from close examination of the various job grading schemes and disciplinary procedure agreements given in the associated documents section. These together with the job descriptions and organisation charts yield enough material for a course on organisational design before moving to the actual disputes.

It is in this area that industrial lawyers will find an interest. Do procedural agreements satisfy the various acts on industrial relations and employee's rights, do the working agreements comply with the Health and Safety at Work Act? The task of re-writing a section of an agreement or a disciplinary procedure by course members can be a most fruitful learning device.

Once students are familiar with industrial relations practice and procedure it is appropriate to move to the case studies in the form of arbitrating on disputes. There are a number of ways in which they may be so used.

One direct way is to role play the situations. In this method two groups take the parts of the management and the other of the employees and unions. The associated documents and perhaps a background note can be given to both sides together with the terms of reference. Further documents or selected information may be given to the union or the management side to support their case. Then a mock hearing can be held with, say, two members of each group acting as spokespersons.

The structure of this exercise can be varied. The tutor can act as arbitrator or one of the participants may act as arbitrator. It can also be run as an arbitration with two assessors, one from the union side, one from management and after the hearing they can debate their decisions before the group. Similarly, the tutor can appoint observers to each group whose task is to observe and analyse the process each group goes through when preparing its case for the hearing. They can also judge whether or not the representatives exceed their brief at the hearing. Afterwards the teams can discuss how they might improve their performance with the observers.

One of the most difficult aspects of any arbitration is the setting of the terms of reference. This is normally done by one of the skilled staff members of ACAS who acts as a conciliator. It is his task to explain and interpret each side's views and attitudes to the other and to attempt to find some suitable agreement. If this is achieved then the dispute has reached a solution through conciliation. However, if this is not possible it is the conciliator's task to encapsulate the difference between the parties as concisely but as neutrally as possible. This is the task of setting the terms of reference and the process can be difficult and exhausting.

Once agreed, the terms of reference should set limits on the outcome of the arbitration. The arbitrator has to find this within the terms of reference even if it is felt that a variation would be preferable. The arbitrator is free to put additional recommendations in his report but his award has to be within the terms of reference.

Role playing an arbitration can be a good learning experience and great fun. More difficult is the setting of terms of reference. One method of doing this is again to give both sides the associated documents and then appropriate material for either the union or the management side. The two sides commence in separate rooms with their respective documents in the usual way. After an hour in which they build their own case the conciliator is introduced. This may well be a small group of three or four persons who have had access to all the information. Their task is to effect a solution through conciliation or if that fails obtain an agreement on terms of reference. It is often found that the terms of reference so produced are quite different from the ones set by ACAS. Here again an instructive discussion can be had about the differences and the accompanying reasons.

At the end of each case study there are a number of questions which will focus on specific and important aspects of the case. The cases are available to be used flexibly and are all based on fact. All the situations are real and have occurred almost exactly as presented. The author has used many of them himself with students, with managers and with shop stewards. The selection presented in this book with backup instructions on the appropriate legal background and guidance with respect to preparing joint agreements between managers and unions should give participants greater understanding of industrial relations theory and practice.

By the end of the course members should be able to participate in industrial relations disputes resolution with greater understanding of the procedures and the law and closer adherence to rational good practice. In this way both sides will benefit, fewer disputes should go through to arbitration and those that do should be better focused and have more specific issues for the arbitrator to judge.

These case studies are suitable for undergraduate students on university courses in personnel management, general management, industrial relations, organisational behaviour, sociology and commercial and industrial law. They may be used on introductory courses to illustrate typical workplace situations without the need for extensive knowledge or analysis. They may also be used towards the end of these courses where students would be required to make comparisons with practice elsewhere and to comment upon the extent to which solutions to the disputes would affect policy and agreements within the company. Law students should be able to state where current practice or the possible solutions to the dispute are affected by current or proposed legislation. Sociology students charting social change should be able to explain how the acceptability of traditional solutions may be affected by changes in social behaviour and cultural attitudes.

Foreign students should find that the disputes described are very similar to the problems which arise in their own countries. They will be expected to prepare solutions that reflect cultural behaviour and legal practice which is usual in their country. For this reason we believe that the problems described are, in a sense, universal and that this book is quite appropriate as a text book in countries other than the United Kingdom.

Mature students, such as middle managers or personnel managers, can use these cases as a basis for discussion at a variety of seminars. Equally, the training and development of union officials can be facilitated by study of the current cases. This would be true at an introductory level for shop steward training or for strategic and policy work for senior managers or union officials concerned with contributing to the organisation's policies on industrial strategy.

The use of these case studies by law students have been mentioned above in the fields of commercial and industrial law. There is another way in which the legal profession might use the cases in this book. Arbitration represents a means of solving disputes in a non-legalistic way. The objective is to frame terms of reference which are sufficiently flexible so that a fair and appropriate solution may be found. It is not the case that legal precedent from a previous age or a legal technicality may force an unfair resolution as sometimes happens under the law. Arbitration avoids those pitfalls and because of this it represents a different way of approaching conflict than the law currently allows.

Legal experts and legal administrators are currently working with other experts in seeking ways to streamline legal procedures and to enhance the justice in the decisions made by courts. One of the processes being examined is ADR, (Alternative Disputes Resolution) of which arbitration is one. The wide range of possible solutions available under arbitration, depending upon the circumstances, can be illustrated by careful use of the cases given in this book. There is no doubt that giving lawyers concerned with developing new legal procedures the opportunity to set terms of reference for arbitration in the cases which follow will guide them to a broader approach to the process of dispensing justice.

A concluding point in the consideration of the use of these case studies is one of time. The disputes described are universal and timeless in any workplace in any country. Consequently the cases should not date in so far as the problem is articulated. It is the frameworks within which solutions may be considered that will vary dependent upon the laws which are in force and the accepted cultural and behavioural norms which exist at the time and place. Consequently, the use of the cases here presented are to a considerable extent multidisciplinary, multinational and universal. It is hoped that teachers, facilitators, students and readers will find them appropriate, useful and interesting.

Part 2

THE CASES

Arbitration between
EASTERN BREWERIES LTD
and
THE PUBLIC HOUSE MANAGERS
ASSOCIATION
(in respect of cash till reconciliation procedures)

Terms of reference

The terms of reference agreed by both parties were:

'The arbitrator to determine whether or not the company has the right to introduce revised procedures in respect of cash control by using the instructions devised by the manufacturers of the cash registers. PHMA on its part consider that as the present system has been used for many years, this proposed change in cash control is unacceptable because it involves a further time factor and will cause problematic work conditions. The Association (PHMA) therefore considers that this be a change and not a revision in the present terms and conditions of employment.'

Documentation

The arbitrator received a full statement of the case from the Public House Managers Association. This was supported by copies of relevant letters and extracts from the minutes of certain Joint Negotiating Committee (JNC) meetings. He also received a comprehensive submission from Eastern Breweries Ltd supported by copies of various agreements between the association and the company, a copy of the contract of employment between the company and its public house managers and a copy of the manufacturer's operating instructions for the till concerned.

Both parties had received and studied each other's submissions.

Background to the dispute

The current dispute between PHMA and Eastern Breweries Ltd has arisen because the company wish to amend the method of operating single entry cash tills which are installed in most of their bars and licensed houses. The majority of cash tills in the company's managed houses are of the single entry type, although there are a few multiple entry tills at some locations.

The amendment requested by the company is that during till reconciliation at the end of a trading session, the manager totals the amounts rung by pressing the 'P' button before the 'Z' button instead of simply pressing the 'Z' button as at present. The union contend that this is a change in reconciliation procedures which will take more time, carries an implied slight on the probity of managers, and that the change is being introduced without due process of negotiation.

The single entry till under consideration is one that has been in use within the company for several years. A particular form of till reconciliation has previously been recommended by the company and is in use in the Western area. In February last year Mr Marshall for the company, discussed the revised till reconciliation procedures with the PHMA paid official, Mr Philip. The company claims that Mr Philip was agreeable to the proposal recognising that it would provide safeguards to all parties. The company then went ahead and attempted to introduce the new procedures in April of that year. The PHMA on behalf of its members claimed that these procedures represented a change and that they had not been negotiated through the JNC and that therefore they were unacceptable. The company then withdrew the proposals.

Since that time there has been some correspondence between the company and the association and the matter has been discussed on several occasions by the JNC. Further delay was occasioned by the fact that the PHMA paid official moved away from the area and was not replaced for several months. During February and April of this year the matter was taken up again by the JNC. Formal notice of dispute was given and the agreed grievance procedure was invoked. The parties failed to agree and the matter was therefore referred to ACAS, who recommended that it should be referred to arbitration.

THE UNION CASE FOR THE ARBITRATOR

The Public House Managers Association

Imperial House
57 Warwick Square
Chesterfield

the arbitrator

Dear Sir

This dispute arose because when we, the JNC, agreed to till reconciliation it was on the pretext that the type we were talking about was the type which was then being used in the Western area within the company, and there was no reason why we should suspect any other system being used. However, the company claim that the type they are introducing is one laid down by the till makers and they see no need to negotiate a procedure with the JNC, even though it obviously has a bearing on a manager's terms and conditions of employment.

First of all it must be said that the JNC on behalf of the managers do not object to till reconciliation as such, but the type the company are introducing is such that it changes the present system so much that we believe the proposed change should have been negotiated paragraph by paragraph with the JNC as would any other changes in terms and conditions of employment.

The company tried to introduce a system of till reconciliation in April of last year without any negotiations with the JNC and it was only following a complaint from our association and a subsequent JNC meeting that the idea was withdrawn, and it is further apparent from the JNC minutes dated 12 April this year that, had we accepted a change in the trading week which was unacceptable, till reconciliation would not have been introduced at all.

The company seem surprised when we state that we are misled when thinking we were accepting the type of till reconciliation that operates in the Western area at the present time, yet I have a letter in my possession from the company dated 30 April last year which states and I quote: 'One has to remember that elsewhere in the region the procedures have been custom and practice for a number of years and we are anxious to avoid any misunderstanding both in the Eastern area and the region generally.'

We submit that bringing in such a system after all the years of custom and practice that have been acceptable to the company is bound to bring problems. It is not as though every house has been issued with new tills, in fact some houses have two different types of till, so it may be arguable there should be two different types of till reconciliation if the procedure is to be one as laid down with the actual piece of equipment.

What is the reason for such an exercise at all? The company state in the JNC minutes dated 16 February this year, and I quote: 'The whole object of the exercise was for the managers to be able to check their daily takings more effectively.' We cannot see such an exercise making any difference to the end result, as no matter what system is used the same amount of money would still be in any given till at the end of any given session.

We would submit that there is absolutely no question that till reconciliation would not stop any misappropriation of till cash and it will not give any added safeguard to managers.

It is quite obvious that when a manager starts to instruct the staff on a new system regarding dealing with cash transactions, that some will view this as a move linked with mistrust and this cannot lead to good industrial relations. Furthermore there are cases where two or three people use the same till so under any system its discrepancies cannot be pin-pointed.

Many of the managers feel this introduction is a direct challenge to their integrity as having been a manager, in some cases for 30 years with the company, they are now being told indirectly that the way they have dealt with their cash and stocks in all that time has not been good enough.

The managers do have a responsible job. First of all it is their job to strike up a relationship with both their customers and staff, and a manager does rely very heavily on a happy working relationship with the staff. The manager is responsible already under his agreement for all stock and cash while working with the company, which in itself is a safeguard of the company's cash and having been given such a responsible job I believe it is up to to the manager to see that the business is run efficiently, as indeed I would submit it has in the majority of cases for many years.

Once again, we must point out there is no objection to the principles of till reconciliation. The objection is to the declaration of cash as instructed in the gross level; this is the procedure that takes the time and also if any error is made in this declaration procedure, e.g. omitting to press the 'P' key or pressing a wrong key while carrying out this declaration procedure, then there will obviously be an error in the total recorded, and this means having to write out explanations of the error even if the cash in the till is correct. The extra time factor in this operation has already been acknowledged by the company by their offer to withdraw the till reconciliation procedure at the end of the lunchtime session. A conservative estimate of the time taken to do one till using the proposed procedure is approximately 15 minutes. (At one of the instruction courses it was confirmed that it took the instructing district manager almost 30 minutes to carry out the procedure on one till.)

It will be seen from this that a manager with two or three tills is going to be involved in seven or ten hours per week over and above his present involvement, and as a manager works at the moment an average of at least 80 hours per week, we feel that this is asking too much. It also poses the problem of carrying out the procedure on a manager's day off.

There is also the question of change of staff using the till during one session (e.g. barman/barmaid opens at 5.30 p.m.). When other staff come in at 7.30–8.00 p.m. they have the right to have a till checked before they start to ascertain that it contains the correct float. This could involve an extra till reconciliation each evening necessitating the till being out of commission for at least 15 minutes in the middle of a trading session.

In the event of a customer querying his correct change, to be able to check whether a £5 or £10 note had been tendered would again involve the same procedure and the till being out of use for a period to the consequent annoyance of the customers at the till in serving.

In conclusion I do not think it is a matter of whether the company has a right to introduce such a system; more the point is whether the company ought to bring in such a system taking into account:

1. That the company has not negotiated those changes in the managers' terms and conditions of employment with the JNC as clearly they should if good industrial relations are to prevail.
2. That it is likely that it will cause relationships between a manager and his staff to be strained by the fact that it may appear that discrepancies have been taking place in the past and now the staff are under scrutiny.
3. A further time factor will be involved eroding away from the manager's rest period.
4. Whether after all these years such an introduction is worth while in view of the fact that the company have stated the exercise is for managers to be able to check their daily takings more effectively, while it is quite obvious it will not be giving any further safeguards to managers whatsoever.

It is our contention that there is already an effective check on the daily takings by the following.

1. Entry on till reconciliation form for each till (duplicate).
2. Similar entry in the daily takings book (triplicate).
3. Cash transactions and totals in tills recorded on till rolls by using the 'Z' key.
4. Regular stock taking and cash checks.
5. The availability of cash at all times for spot checks by the district manager or other officials.

We firmly believe that such a change would be a significant alteration in terms and conditions, and I feel sure that the type of till reconciliation that was in operation in the Western area at the time of our acceptance at JNC level would be sufficient for both parties in that it would:

(a) bring uniformity throughout Eastern Breweries Ltd and
(b) it would give the company the till readings of the dinner time and closing sections, etc., which I believe is what the company really requires.

Signed

F. Norman
Regional Organiser
The Public House Managers Association

THE COMPANY CASE FOR THE ARBITRATOR

1. The employers: Eastern Breweries Ltd
Meldrum House
Vine Street
Chesterfield

Represented by: 1. Mr P. Marshall, chairman of the JNC and regional managing director of Eastern Breweries Ltd.

2. Mr A. D. Ritchie, joint secretary of the JNC and an employee relations adviser employed by Eastern Breweries Ltd with specific responsibilities for the public house operation.

Eastern Breweries Ltd forms part of the Eastern and Northern group of companies. It has an area of operation roughly covering Yorkshire and Lancashire. In view of the fact that it is a distribution, wholesale and retailing business, rather than a production operation, the region is split into two selling areas: i.e. Eastern and Western. Each of these has its own managing director who is responsible to the company managing director.

2. The employees

All public house managers employed by Eastern Breweries Ltd are within scope of a Post Entry Union Membership and Procedural Arrangement signed by the company and the PHMA.

PHMA was originally granted a Recognition and Procedural Agreement with the company in June 1972. By 1973 the association had achieved the right to negotiate the rates of pay, and terms and conditions of employment for its members.

The Substantive Agreement, however, was and still is complementary to the Individual Manager's Contract of Service, Appendix 1.

3. The matter in dispute

The company's insistence that the managers carry out till reconciliation in accordance with the instruction issued by the cash till manufacturers, as a further aid to cash control.

4. Mutually agreed terms of reference

The arbitrator to determine whether or not the company has the right to introduce revised procedures in respect of cash control by using the instructions devised by the manufacturers of the cash registers.

PHMA, on its part, considers that as the present system has been used for many years, this proposed change in cash control is unacceptable because it involves a further time factor and will cause problematic work conditions. The association therefore considers that this be a change and not a revision in the present terms and conditions of employment.

5. The company case

The company considers that it is right and proper to be able to account for all monies it receives resulting from cash sales in its public house section. The company furthermore believes that the introduction of till reconciliation would help to protect not only its public house managers but also the employees employed therein where they are involved with the direct handling of cash.

It is the company's further belief that to assist its 250 managers who employ some 2000 staff to retail the company's products to its customers, it must install effective control equipment for cash and that having done so it would be extremely foolish not to introduce the manufacturers' recommended procedures when using that equipment.

The company recognises that in order to use such equipment effectively, it is necessary to ensure that its employees are properly trained in its use. This has been done to the satisfaction of the company and PHMA (*see* Appendix 2).

The licensees must be fully aware that in their contractual agreements' clauses (*see* Appendix 1) it is stated:

6.(i)   to carry out company rules
6.(j)   to permit inspection of books
8.   to account for all monies received

The company would be within their rights to terminate any individual agreement for non-compliance with the proper use of company accounting methods using the equipment provided.

In fact in February last year when Mr P. R. Marshall first consulted with PHMA, the company indicated at that time the improved tills would give safeguards to all parties, and this was not disputed by the PHMA paid official.

The company, having spent considerable sums of money in consulting with the licensees on this subject, are shocked that the licensees have seen fit to pursue this simple instruction to arbitration. Furthermore, they are perturbed that agreements entered into openly by both parties should be disregarded within 12 months. On 12 April last year the company withdrew from its wish to change the trading week, on the understanding that the till reconciliation exercise would be introduced on a company basis.

ASSOCIATED DOCUMENTS

Minutes of the PHMA Joint Negotiating Committee held in Meldrum House at 10.30 a.m. on 16 February this year

Present:

Management:
P. R. Marshall – Chairman
W. D. Jolly
A. D. Ritchie – Joint Secretary

PHMA:
A. Barker – Chairman
W. Hague
J. Martin
R. Peters
J. Williams
C. Arnott – Joint Secretary

The chairman, Mr P. R. Marshall, welcomed the delegates to the newly constituted JNC which had been formed consequent upon the reorganisation within Eastern Breweries Ltd.

Minutes of the previous meeting

The minutes of the meeting held on 19 August were read and approved.

Matters arising

m1   Post entry closed shop

It was agreed that this matter should be ongoing but could not proceed until such time as either a full time paid official of PHMA had been appointed or that Mr Arnott was able to receive some assistance from his headquarters.

m3   Till reconciliation

It was agreed that further consultation at local level should proceed on this matter.

Mr Hague stated that he and his members were against the implementation of till reconciliation.

Mr Marshall stated that he thought these views to be wrong. A manager left himself open to criticism and the whole object of the exercise was for the managers to be able to check their daily takings more effectively.

m7   House evaluation

It was agreed that this matter was ongoing but should be left in abeyance until the further pay restraint policy was clear.

m5 Calculation of staff wages from centre

The chairman and his colleagues would consider this point at board level and report back at the next meeting of the JNC.

m7 Notification of vacancies

Mr R. Peters complained that houses were still being offered without other PHMA members being considered. He was specific in naming two: 'The Brown Cow' and 'The Red Lion' at Corley.

Minutes of the PHMA Joint Negotiating Committee held in Meldrum House at 10.30 a.m. on 12 April this year

Present:

Management:	PHMA:
P. R. Marshall – Chairman	A. Barker – Chairman
W. D. Jolly	W. Hague
A. D. Ritchie – Joint Secretary	J. Williams
	R. Peters
	C. Arnott – Joint Secretary
	F. Norman – Joint Secretary

Apologies

Mr J. Martin sent his apologies.

New PHMA organiser

Mr C. Arnott who had been acting regional secretary introduced Mr F. Norman who had been appointed as regional secretary for PHMA.

Mr C. Arnott

Mr P. R. Marshall expressed the company's and delegates' thanks to Mr Arnott who once again carried out the duties of the regional secretary for PHMA.

Minute 12 – change in trading week

Mr Arnott stated that the meeting had been called because it was the general opinion, resulting from the previous JNC meeting, that any change in the trading week would not be acceptable to the membership.

Mr Marshall pointed out that he had been continuously raising the question of cash security with the managers' representatives over the last 12 months. Recent events have proved that there was a greater need to control the cash and therefore the change in the trading week had been introduced to improve the cash controls.

The delegates pointed out that management had failed in its disciplines, furthermore the facilities were there to discipline individuals who failed in their obligations.

Mr Marshall finally proposed that if the introduction of till reconciliation could be adopted as a company procedure and regular cash spot checks be carried out by district sales managers, the company were prepared to retain the trading week Sunday to Saturday.

Adjournment

Upon resumption Mr Arnott confirmed that the company proposals had been fully discussed and they were recommending that the membership accept the proposals. He also asked the company to ensure that the district sales managers adequately trained managers in the work involved in till reconciliation. In addition he requested that the company should review its training procedures to ensure that entrants fully understood all the managers' duties.

Public House Managers Association

Imperial House
57 Warwick Square
Chesterfield
28 April

RP/CP

Eastern Breweries Ltd
Meldrum House
Vine Street
Chesterfield

For the attention of Mr A. D. Ritchie

Dear Mr Ritchie

re: Introducing of paperwork titled 'Till sheet and till reconciliation' distributed to managers

I have today attended a meeting in Chesterfield of the Eastern area managers, and it was brought to my attention that the company, without prior discussion or negotiation, have introduced paperwork relative to the above, which I am given to understand was attempted some three years ago or thereabouts and which at that time was not implemented by the managers.

I am rather surprised, in view of the recent problem relative to the walk-in stocktaking, that the company should introduce changes in methods of work without prior consultation.

I therefore write to inform you, without prejudice to any further discussions you may wish to have on the subject, that the managers in the Eastern area have been advised not to participate in this exercise and, in addition, I have written to each of our representatives on the JNC informing them of this position.

Yours faithfully

Richard Philip
Eastern Regional Organiser

Eastern Breweries Ltd

Meldrum House
Vine Street
Chesterfield

Ref: ADR/CRT

29 April

R. Philip, Esq.
Public House Managers Association
Imperial House
57 Warwick Square
Chesterfield

Dear Mr Philip

Eastern area managers – grievance

I am in receipt of your letter dated 28 April in respect of a reported grievance to you concerning till sheets and till reconciliation sheets. That this matter has been raised in such a manner is to say the least disconcerting, in view of the fact that only seven days previously a meeting of the Eastern Area Consultative Committee was held with management and that at no stage in the proceedings was the concern raised by the members.

In view of the harmonious relationships that we have enjoyed in the past with the Eastern area managers, we fail to understand why they have at no stage raised this matter locally. There is an historical record of discussion of which you may be unaware and therefore I would recommend that in accordance with our existing procedures, this matter should be dealt with at local level rather than JNC level. One has to remember that elsewhere in the region, the procedures have been custom and practice for a number of years and we are anxious to avoid any misunderstanding, both in the Eastern area and the region generally.

Perhaps your secretary would be good enough to contact Mr W. Bond at Port Street who is the divisional director responsible for this area – in order that we can arrange an early meeting with yourself and the Eastern Area Committee.

Yours faithfully
EASTERN BREWERIES

A. D. Ritchie
Employee Relations Adviser

Appendix 1

Individual Manager's Contract of Service

This Agreement is made the   day of one thousand nine hundred and   Between Eastern Breweries Ltd whose registered office is at Meldrum House, Chesterfield (hereinafter called 'the Company') of the one part and

(hereinafter called 'the Manager') of the other part subject to the Manager obtaining a full transfer of the Licences relating to the premises it is hereby agreed as follows:

1. The Manager shall serve the Company and the Company shall employ the Manager to manage all the business of a licensed victualler at the premises described in the Schedule hereto (in this Agreement called 'the Premises') from the commencing date specified in the Schedule. He shall give the whole of his attention to such business and use his best endeavours to improve the business and if required shall reside on the Premises and shall not without the consent of the Company in writing:
   (a) Be interested in or concerned with any other business.
   (b) Accept office or act as treasurer or any other officer of any society or club other than a trade union or association connected with the licensed trade.
   (c) Use or hold out or permit to be used or held out the name of the Company or any representative or employee of the Company in connection with or as responsible for any such society or club.
2. (a) The Company shall during this Agreement pay to the Manager the salary and other benefits specified in the Schedule hereto at the times and in the manner set out in the Schedule.
   (b) The Manager shall be entitled to the holiday details of which are set out in the Schedule hereto to be taken at a time agreed with the Company and shall be entitled to such other holiday as the Company shall allow. The Manager shall be entitled to holiday pay in lieu of holiday on the terms set out in the schedule hereto.
   (c) If the Manager shall be ill and be unable to work he shall send a medical certificate to the Company on the third day of such illness and such subsequent certificates as may be required. The Company's sick pay scheme currently in force shall become operative after the third day of illness. A copy of such Scheme is held by the Company's District Manager and is available for inspection on request. Such copy will have any future changes entered up in it or be replaced by a copy containing such changes.

(d) The Manager shall work such hours as may be necessary for the proper performance of his duties.

(e) The Manager shall be entitled to one rest day each week to be taken on a day to be agreed with the Company.

(f) The Manager shall join and maintain membership of the Company's pension scheme currently in force. A copy of such a scheme is held by the Company's District Manager and is available for inspection on request. Such copy will have any future changes entered up in it or be replaced by a copy containing such changes.

(g) This Agreement may be terminated by the Company given in writing to the Manager the notice as specified in the Schedule thereto or by the Manager giving to the Company four weeks notice in writing.

(h) Any notice given to the Manager shall be properly given if left at or sent by Recorded Delivery to the Manager at the premises.

(i) The Manager shall have the right to be a member of such Registered Trade Union as he may choose and to take part in its activities and if elected to hold office.

(j) The Manager shall also have the right to refuse to be a member of a Registered Trade Union Association or Unregistered Organisation of Workers or any particular Trade Union Association or Organisation of Workers.

(k) If an Agency Shop Agreement is in force which applied to the Manager he will be notified by the Company together with the manner in which such an Agency Shop Agreement will affect the Manager should he decide to exercise his right under Paragraph (j) of this Clause.

3. A copy of the Company's Grievance Procedure is held by the Company's District Manager and is available for inspection on request. Such copy will have any future changes entered up in it or be replaced by a copy containing such changes.

4. (a) The Manager together with his wife and dependent children (if any) shall occupy any accommodation provided on the Premises free of charge. This shall not constitute a tenancy of the Premises and such occupation shall be for the proper performance of his duties and as a servant of the Company and shall come to an end with the determination of the Manager's service.

(b) The Manager shall not without the consent of the Company in writing lend or let residential accommodation in the Premises either temporarily or permanently to any person whatsoever.

(c) The Company shall not be responsible for loss or damage to the Manager's furniture or personal effects caused by fire theft or other accident.

5. The Manager has deposited with the Company the sum specified in the Schedule (in this Agreement called 'the deposit') which will be held by the Company on the following terms:

    (a) The Company shall be at liberty during or at the determination of the Agreement to use all or part of the deposit in making good any deficiencies in the stock or money or fixtures or fittings or utensils or other effects of the Company unless the Manager can show to the reasonable satisfaction of the Company that such a deficiency arose through no fault or neglect on his part.

    (b) The Company shall pay interest on such sum or on so much thereof as shall not have been applied by the Company in accordance with Paragraph (a) of this Clause at a rate equal to Bank Rate in force on the first day of the Company's current financial year.

    (c) The deposit or so much as shall remain after the Company has applied any part of it in accordance with Paragraph (a) of this Clause shall be repaid to the Manager together with all interest due within thirty days of the end of the Manager's service with the Company provided that the Manager shall have:

        (i) given up to the Company possession of the Premises

        (ii) signed all Notices and

        (iii) taken all other action required by the Company to secure the transfer of the Justices Licence permitting the sale of intoxicants from the Premises all extensions thereof any music and dancing licence any permit or excise licence relating to any gaming machine and all other licences or permits relating to the Premises (in this Agreement called 'the Licences') to the Company or to whom it may direct.

6. The Manager agrees with the Company:

    (a) To conduct and manage the Premises in a proper and orderly manner and in conformity with the law.

    (b) To keep the Premises open during all permitted hours for the sale and consumption of intoxicating liquor unless otherwise permitted in writing by the Company.

    (c) To supply food for sale upon the Premises when required by the Company so to do.

    (d) Not to permit or suffer any betting or unlawful gaming on the Premises.

    (e) Not to do or suffer any other things to be done on the Premises result of which the Licence may be forfeited or suspended or placed in jeopardy in any way whatsoever and to comply with all conditions or undertakings attached to the Licences or given to the Licensing Justices.

    (f) To give immediate notice to the Company of any of the following matters:

(i) of any requirement or complaint made or warning given to him by any Police Officer or Officer of Excise or by or on behalf of the Licensing Justices in respect of his conduct of the business carried on at the Premises and of any summons issued against him in respect of any offence charge against him in respect of his conduct as a licence holder or otherwise

(ii) of any person having been to his knowledge convicted of any offence committed upon the Premises or having been apprehended on the charge of committing any such offence or having been served with any summons in respect thereof

(iii) of any notice or complaint received by him from any local authority as to the sanitary condition of the Premises or their fitness for habitation or use

(iv) of any request to give an undertaking relating to the Premises or the Licences

(v) of any communication affecting the interest of the Company.

(g) To apply for Licences or renewal or transfer thereof or Protection Order as requested by the Company to give all necessary notices and do all acts or deeds necessary to obtain the Licences and to deal with the Licences as he may be directed by the Company.

(h) Not to apply for an occasional licence without the consent of the Company.

(i) To acquaint himself with the Company's rules and regulations and at all times to see that they are carried out and further to comply with all directions given from time to time by the Company.

(j) To produce and to permit the Company to inspect and if required remove all the books papers letters documents cash and stock relating to the Premises and business thereof which may be in the possession or under the control of the Manager and to permit the Company to have all access to all parts of the Premises for any purpose connected with the business including the checking of cash and stock in trade and the Company's furnishings and loose effects.

(k) To take charge of and preserve in good order and condition (fair wear and tear excepted) all fixtures fittings furniture and utensils of the Company which at any time are on the Premises and deliver up to the Company the same in such state at the end of this agreement.

(l) To inspect so far as he reasonably can all parts of the Premises at regular intervals and to notify the Company forthwith of any defects in or repairs needed to the Premises and to keep the Premises and all drains toilet accommodation and all sinks draining boards glasses and other equipment and utensils including beer dispense equipment scrupulously clean and in good order and condition and to keep the Premises clean and tidy and to keep the garden grounds or other surround neat and tidy.

(m) To permit the Company to inspect the whole of the Premises including the living accommodation (if any) thereat at all reasonable times.

(n) Not in any way whatsoever to adulterate any of the liquor or other commodities for sale in or upon the Premises.

(o) Only to order display or sell goods in accordance with the directions of the Company and from the sources nominated by the Company to supply the same. The selling of such goods to be at prices from time to time directed by the Company and no credit shall be granted for the sale of intoxicating liquor unless supplied either for consumption with a meal supplied at the same time or for consumption by a person residing in the Premises or his guests.

(p) Not to pledge the credit of the Company on any account whatsoever nor to enter into any contract on behalf of the Company without the express permission in writing of the Company.

(q) Not to divulge to any person at any time unless expressly authorised by the Company any information as to the conduct management or dealings of the business nor to permit any other person so to do and not without the authorisation of the Company to give interviews to or make comments on such matters to any newspaper radio or television representative.

7. The Manager shall out of the monies received by him in the course of the business pay the assistants and servants employed in the business such wages and salaries in accordance with any regulations governing the same for the time being in force and in accordance with such rates as from time to time may be notified to him by the Company. The Manager shall comply with all statutory and Company rules and regulations relating to the employment of servants or assistants so far as the same apply to the servants or assistants employed on the Premises and shall be responsible for the deduction of income tax and the stamping of National Insurance Cards.

8. The Manager shall pay the rest of all the monies received by him in the course of the business into such Bank as the Company shall direct and such payments to such Bank shall be made at least three times in each week or as the Company shall direct. The Manager shall account to the Company for all monies received by him.

9.   (a)   On the determination of the engagement of the Manager he shall without further consideration pecuniary or otherwise sign all notices and make all attendance and do all acts or things necessary for transferring the Licences held by him to such person or persons as the Company may direct.

      (b)   In case the Manager shall on request of the Company refuse or shall neglect to renew the Licence or transfer the same as herein mentioned or to join with the Company in making application for the removal of the Licences it shall be lawful for the Company which is hereby irrevocably empowered by the Manager to do all things necessary to effect such renewal transfer or removal and for such purposes to sign and document for and on behalf of and in the name of the Manager and to appear before the Justices either personally or by its solicitors or agents to apply for such renewal and to consent as the agent of the Manager to a transfer being made to a new licensee of the Premises. It shall be lawful for the Company at its expense and it is hereby irrevocably empowered by the Manager in his name to appeal against any order made to renew transfer or remove the Licences or against any order made in respect of the Premises and do all acts and things necessary or proper in respect of such appeal.

10.   This Agreement shall cease immediately on any of the following events.

      (a)   The death of the Manager.

      (b)   If the Manager shall take leave of absence from the Premises without the consent of the Company.

      (c)   If the Manager shall have a Receiving Order in Bankruptcy made against him.

      (d)   If the renewal of any of the Licences shall be refused to him.

      (e)   If the Manager shall commit a breach of or shall not perform any of the agreements on his part contained or referred to in this Agreement or shall in the opinion of the Company commit any act or default whereby any of the Licences shall be placed in jeopardy or if the Manager shall in the opinion of the Company be guilty of gross misconduct. It is expressly agreed and declared between the parties hereto that the decision of the Company as to whether the Licences shall have been placed in jeopardy or endangered by any act or default of the Manager or whether the Manager shall have been guilty of gross misconduct shall be binding and conclusive as between the parties hereto.

      (f)   Upon the Manager attaining the age of 65 years or 60 years if a female.

Upon the termination of this Agreement the Manager his wife and family shall immediately vacate the premises.

11. Nothing herein contained shall be construed as in any sense creating a partnership between the Company and the Manager.
12. This Agreement constitutes written particulars of the Manager's Employment under the Contracts of Employment Act 1963 as amended.
13. In this Agreement where the context so requires words importing the masculine gender only shall include the feminine.

As Witness the hands of the parties the day and year above written.

Schedule above referred to

CLAUSE IN AGREEMENT	WORD	DEFINITION
1.	Premises	
1.	Commencing Date	
2.(a)	Salary and Method of payment	
(i.e. £	per annum paid	weekly monthly etc.)
2.(b)	Summary of other benefits	
2.(c)	Holiday	3 weeks during the period 1 January to 31 December in each calendar year to be taken at a time agreed with the Company
		Days in lieu of Public and Bank Holidays shall be taken at a time agreed with the Company
		On completion of years' service in the holiday year the Manager will be entitled to four weeks holiday in that and subsequent years

CLAUSE IN   WORD   DEFINITION
AGREEMENT

On commencing employment
during the current holiday year
the Manager will receive holidays
as set out below:

Total service which can be
completed by 31 December

Less than 3 months   week(s)

3 months but less than 6 months
     week(s)

6 months but less than 9 months
     week(s)

Over 9 months   week(s)

A Manager who joins during a
holiday year shall receive his full
holiday entitlement from the
beginning of the following
holiday year.

On ceasing to be employed by
the Company the Manager shall
receive holiday entitlement as
follows:

Holidays already taken shall be
deducted from the entitlement.

Completed service in holiday
year to date of leaving

Three Week   Four Week
Entitlement   Entitlement

Less than 3 months
     week(s)   weeks(s)

CLAUSE IN AGREEMENT	WORD	DEFINITION
		3 months but less than 6 months week(s) weeks(s)
		6 months but less than 9 months week(s) weeks(s)
		Over 9 months week(s) week(s)
2 (b)	Holiday Pay	Payment in lieu of holiday will be made in accordance with the above entitlements
2 (g)	Notice to terminate	Up to 10 years service by the Manager — 4 weeks
		10–15 years service by the Manager — 6 weeks
		After 15 years service by the Manager — 8 weeks
5.	The Deposit	£

Signed by

    on behalf of the Company
    in the presence of:

Signed by the Manager

in the presence of:

I acknowledge that I have received a copy of this Agreement

        (the within-named Manager)

        dated   19

Appendix 2

Princess Single-entry Register

Instructions for the system of the declaration of cash – decimal mode

At the end of trading and at the last sale, carry out the following cashing up procedure:

1. Wind down audit roll to a clear space. Write in the autographic window the time (i.e. 5.35 p.m.).
2. Open the cash drawer by depressing the total bar only; this will print a row of zeros on audit roll (and the non-reset '10,000' counter will advance by one digit) as shown below:

1234   00.00

3. Count the cash in the drawer inserts and deduct the opening float to arrive at the net total of cash takings (e.g. £656.94).
4. Declare this total on the register, using the following procedure:
   Firstly depress 'P' button followed by amount keys £6.56 and depress total bar. (The non-reset '10,000' counter will advance by one digit). This will record on audit roll thus:

1235   06.56   P

   The odd 94p should be recorded by again depressing the 'P' button and amount keys for 94p and depressing the total bar. This will record on audit roll as follows (the non-reset '10,000' counter will advance by one digit):

1236   00.94   P

   This then completes the 'declaration'.
5. Now insert the 'Z' key (adjacent to 'Z' button). When this is turned, the grand total reset counter is automatically advanced by one digit in the window below the 'Z' button. Depress 'Z' button and total bar. The non-reset '10,000' counter will advance by one digit and the grand total is recorded on audit roll thus:

1237   652.34   Z

Do not restore 'Z' key yet!

6. Either remove section of audit roll or wind down existing section to a clear space.

7. Depress total bar again to produce a row of zeros (proof that machine grand total is cleared). The non-reset counter will advance by one. Write the date on the audit roll. The register is now ready for use.

Withdraw 'Z' key

8. Write above the date on the audit roll, the grand total reset reading showing in the window.

   The audit roll should read thus:

   0026
   25/6/69
   1238   00.00   Z

Below is an example of a correctly completed audit roll showing consecutive operation:

0026
25/6/69
1238   00.00   Z

1237 652.34   Z
1236   00.94   P
1235   06.56   P
1234   00.00   .

5.35 p.m.

It will clearly be seen that this audit roll shows up an 'over' of £4.60 in the cash drawer.

Appendix 3

Till reconciliation sheet

1	2	3	4	5	6	7
	Actual cash in till	Paid out on bottles	Till reading	Over	Under	Remarks
	£ p		£ p			

Instructions for completion of till reconciliation sheet for use with Princess Single-entry Register

1. Complete the declaration of cash as explained in the leaflet attached.
2. Enter cash declared on the till reconciliation sheet under Column 2 (headed 'actual cash in till').
3. Take reading from till and enter under Column 4 (headed 'till reading').
4. Record under Column 3 (marked 'paid out on bottles') any refunds made for bottles returned where cash has been taken out of the till.
5. If cash in till (Column 2) exceeds 'till reading' (Column 4) record the difference in Column 5 (headed 'over').
6. If the cash in till (Column 2) is less than till reading (Column 4) record the difference in Column 6 (headed 'under').
7. Column 7 ('remarks'). Explanations of any items incorrectly rung through the till which may account for the unders or overs.

This procedure is to be adopted every session and the till sheet passed to the stocktaker at each stock. The stocktaker will pass fresh till sheets for each till.

The cash register tills are exclusively for recording sales of all items made on behalf of the company, and cash taken for catering or other sundry items not contained in the company stocks (belonging to the manager) must *not* be included in any cash register transactions. All monies rung through tills are taken to be the property of the company.

Any malfunctions of the cash registers must be reported to the district office immediately, who will arrange servicing.

Should the engineer's service be required to the register, any transactions recorded by him, on a test basis, must be initialled by him at opening/closing of test.

On no account must the cash register drawer be left open during the hours of trading and staff must be instructed to close the drawer after each order. All company transactions must be rung through the till.

Total 'actual cash in till' (Column 2) must equal the total takings recorded on the WSOB for the stocktaking period.

Questions

1 Do you consider that the change in the procedure of till reconciliation is sufficient to require full re-negotiation of the agreement?

2 In view of the opposition of the Public House Managers Association and the possible alienation of the managers do you think it wise for Eastern Breweries Ltd to pursue the proposed changes?

3 Do you think Eastern Breweries Ltd should have engaged in more consultation before introducing the changes?

Arbitration between
SMITHS CHEMICALS LTD
and
the BLACKSMITHS and MILLWRIGHTS UNION
(in respect of argon arc welding)

Terms of reference

The terms of reference agreed by both parties were:

'The arbitrator is asked to resolve an issue concerning argon arc welding at the Company's Bristol plant. The difference turns on who should carry out this type of welding. The Blacksmiths and Millwrights Union argues that its rights to the work has already been established and should be continued. The company does not agree and wishes to retain flexibility to have the work carried out by members of other craft unions, if required.'

Documentation

The arbitrator received a statement of the case from the Blacksmiths and Millwrights Union. He also received a comprehensive submission from Smiths Chemicals Ltd, together with a Statement of Agreement reached between Smiths Chemicals Ltd and the Blacksmiths and Millwrights Union concerning temporary arrangements during the period of the dispute.

The arbitrator also received a request from the Association of Coppersmiths and the Engineering Workers Union for an informal meeting. In addition, a written statement was received from the Association of Coppersmiths.

Both parties to the dispute received and studied each other's submissions.

Background to the dispute

Smiths Chemicals Ltd is a major producer of polyester chemicals. The company has a total of 540 employees of whom 88 are hourly paid engineering maintenance workers. The maintenance work required the use of welding processes for fabrication. Oxy-acetylene welding is widely used for these purposes, but a certain amount of welding has been done using the argon arc process. Until now argon arc welding has been conducted by members of the Blacksmiths and Millwrights Union although there is some evidence to indicate that on occasions outside contractors have used this method of welding when they have been hired by the company for specific items of maintenance.

The greater part of the welding carried out on the company's premises is oxy-acetylene welding. The welders employed by the company are variously members of the Blacksmiths and Millwrights Union, the Association of Coppersmiths and the Engineering Workers Union. For reasons of technological development an increasing amount of fabrication previously welded by the oxy-acetylene method will in future be welded by the argon arc process. The dispute centres on whether or not the Blacksmiths and Millwrights Union should have exclusive right to do this work. The matter is compounded by the fact that welders employed by the other two unions, who are skilled in the oxy-acetylene method, would have to undergo a short course of training to equip them for argon arc welding, and the fact that the company has taken steps to provide this training.

THE UNION CASE TO THE ARBITRATOR

Blacksmiths and Millwrights Union

Avon District
47 Ferry Road
Bristol

Dear Sir

I submit the following points for your consideration which are relative to the forthcoming arbitration to be held at Smiths Chemicals Ltd, Bristol.

Members of my union, the BMU, have been employed at Smiths Chemicals Ltd for at least 60 years. During this period they alone have been responsible for all welding involving the use of arc welding and argon arc welding.

I feel it is unnecessary to go too far back in time and I will refer to instances concerning the erection of new plant and the maintenance of older plant during recent years.

(a)   The extension to the Polyester Plant in 1974 during which all argon arc welding and arc welding was done by members of the BMU.

(b)   The installation of No. 3 splitting column in 1975 involved the use of argon arc welding. This welding was done exclusively by the BMU who were employed by Hatton Engineering contractors, but under the supervision of Smiths Chemicals Ltd management.

(c)   During the course of the Thiokol contract in 1976, Hatton Engineering attempted to bring a welder from another union on to the contract. Mr B. Meriden, BMU Shop Steward, complained to Smiths Chemicals management, which resulted in Mr S. Willis, Smiths Personnel Manager, visiting the site and issuing instructions to Hatton Engineering management that only members of the BMU were to do the welding. The reason Mr S. Willis gave for his decision was that it was in keeping with the site practice.

(d)   Repairs to the polyester plant during April 1979 involved stainless steel welding by the argon arc process on burst coils. The West Bristol Construction Company carried out the contract. This work was done entirely by the BMU on the insistence of Mr B. Clifford, Smiths Chemicals Ltd, Chief Engineer over maintenance.

(e)   During the early part of 1980 work on the dual feeder concerning argon arc welding on a stainless steel hopper was carried out by welder members of the BMU.

In the above submissions I have attempted, very briefly, to highlight certain instances which I consider immediate to the current problem. There are other instances not referred to but which must be documented in the management files and could be helpful at the hearing.

In conclusion, I must state that the management's claim rests solely on a reference to the Donovan Engineering undertaking repairs to an aluminium tank in 1978. They say a non-BMU welder employed by the Donovan company operated the argon arc. I claim that this did not happen and submit the following as a factual account of the event.

Mr B. Meriden, BMU Shop Steward was sent to argon arc the aluminium tank but unfortunately had no argon box to complete the job. Because of this Mr B. Meriden agreed that Donovan be brought in on the basis that the welder was a BMU member. The Donovan company's welder produced and showed Mr Meriden his BMU card. He completed the job within 15 minutes and left the site.

C. Tiffen
Avon District Delegate
Blacksmiths and Millwrights Union

THE COMPANY CASE TO THE ARBITRATOR

Smiths Chemicals Ltd

Briefing document for arbitrator

General background to the dispute

1. Smiths Chemicals Ltd is a major producer of polyester chemicals. The company has a total of 540 employees, of whom 88 are hourly paid engineering maintenance workers, including three employed as coppersmiths, two as sheet metal workers and four as blacksmiths. Of the three coppersmiths, two are members of the Association of Coppersmiths, and the other is a member of the Engineering Workers Union. The engineering trade unions represented on site are:

    AUEW – Amalgamated Union of Engineering Workers
    EWU – Engineering Workers Union
    BMU – Blacksmiths & Millwrights Union
    AC – Association of Coppersmiths
    TGWU – Transport & General Workers Union

2. For many years welding of stainless steel by employees of the Company has been carried out by the coppersmiths and blacksmiths.

    Fabrication of stainless steel pipework by employees of the company is, by custom and practice, carried out by coppersmiths, and for certain duties, pipework below 6 in. diameter has been completely welded by coppersmiths using the oxy-acetylene technique. For other more stringent process duties, stainless steel pipework fabricated by copper-smiths and 'tack welded' by them using oxy-acetylene techniques, is welded by the blacksmiths using open arc 'stick' welding, which gives a higher corrosion resistance than oxy-acetylene welding. The decision as to which technique is to be used for a particular job is made by Engineering Department Management on technical grounds related to corrosion resistance and to process conditions of temperature, pressure, chemical exposure, etc.

3. Argon arc welding has, on several occasions, been used on the company sites by BMU welders employed by the company and by members of the AC employed by an outside contractor. Overall, however, the use of the technique has hitherto not been in general use.

    In view of the increasing demand for greater reliability of process pipe-work, the company's engineering management recently recognised the technical advantages in replacing the use of oxy-acetylene welding with argon arc welding for stainless steel pipework, i.e. less weld cracking, avoidance of oxidisation at the weld, and improved corrosion resistance.

The current dispute

1. Following consultation with the Coppersmiths Association on 25 April, they agreed to the Company's proposal to replace their use of oxy-acetylene welding with argon arc welding. An external training course was, therefore, arranged for the 18/19 May and an order was placed for the necessary equipment.

2. At a meeting on 9 May the blacksmiths informed the company that they were not prepared to accept coppersmiths using the argon arc welding technique at Smiths Chemicals. The following elements were claimed:

    (a) that as a result of custom and practice, the use of argon arc welding at Smiths Chemicals was the sole prerogative of blacksmiths;

    (b) that the blacksmiths had not been consulted prior to introducing this technique to the coppersmiths' work;

    (c) that as a result of the use of argon arc welding by coppersmiths the blacksmiths would lose a substantial volume of work and would then 'only have work passed to them by courtesy of the coppersmiths'. Thus their earnings and security of their employment at Smiths Chemicals was threatened;

    (d) that as the current sole users of open arc 'stick' welding, they were entitled to the exclusive use of argon arc welding which also used an electrical heat source;

    (e) that the training course arranged for the coppersmiths must be cancelled prior to further discussions.

At this meeting the company rejected the blacksmiths' claim for exclusive rights to argon arc welding, but offered to discuss any reasonable concern for their level of earnings or their security of employment. Owing to the ample opportunity for discussion before argon arc welding could be implemented by coppersmiths, and to the long delay (four months) in obtaining alternative training, the company refused to cancel the training course arranged. As a result, the blacksmiths immediately went on strike in support of their claim.

3. The company rejected the claim at this time on the following grounds:

    (a) argon arc welding is a technique widely used in industry, both locally and nationally, by a number of trade unions, including the AC and EWU;

    (b) the fact that at Smiths Chemicals only blacksmiths use open arc 'stick' welding did not confer an automatic right to argon arc welding, a completely different technique;

    (c) The occasional, sporadic incidence of argon arc welding at Smiths Chemicals by blacksmiths fell drastically short of an exclusive well established 'custom and practice';

    (d)   the blacksmiths were given a categoric assurance that ample work existed for blacksmiths and that no reduction in the number of blacksmiths employed would arise as a result of this proposal;

    (e)   in using this technique, the coppersmiths would only be carrying out their existing work using a different technique. As this would not impinge upon the blacksmiths' work, it had not been considered necessary to involve the blacksmiths in prior consultation.

4.   During the period 10–31 May, a series of discussions were held between the company and the union in an attempt to reach interim agreement on a return to normal working by the blacksmiths, and on a basis for a resolution to the dispute. In order to facilitate this, the company offered to defer the implementation of argon arc welding by the company's coppersmiths on factory breakdown, maintenance and capital investment work pending a resolution of the dispute, and to confine their role with argon arc welding to practical training on test pieces not associated with 'live' factory work.

The parties failed to reach agreement during these meetings principally because the company considered they were unable to give the additional undertaking required by BMU that no outside company would be allowed to employ other than BMU members on argon arc welding on the company site. This undertaking was refused by the company on the grounds that:

    (a)   such work had already, on occasions in the past, been carried out on site by a local contractor using AC tradesmen;

    (b)   urgent work was foreseen in the near future for which the company would again require the particular skill and experience in argon arc welding known to be available from this contractor.

5.   Having failed to reach agreement, the company and the union agreed, on 31 May, to seek the assistance of a conciliation officer of ACAS. Following discussion with the company and the union, the conciliator confirmed the view of the parties that a resolution of the argon arc welding dispute was likely to be achieved only by the involvement of an independent arbitrator to be appointed by ACAS.

6.   As a pre-requisite to arbitration, the union insisted upon a return to work by their members. In order to facilitate this, the company undertook to defer, by some months, argon arc welding work planned for the two week factory shutdown, which would otherwise again have been carried out by the outside contractor who has, in the past, carried out this work and who employs members of AC for this purpose.

This allowed the parties to agree to a return to work by the blacksmiths on an interim compromise basis which included the provision that no argon arc welding would be carried out on the site by any outside contractor pending the outcome of the arbitration.

7. Following the claim by BMU to exclusive rights to the use of the argon arc welding technique at Smiths Chemicals Ltd, the District Secretaries of both the Coppersmiths Union and the EWU were contacted by their respective members employed as coppersmiths at Smiths Chemicals Ltd. The work of these employees includes a substantial volume of oxy-acetylene welding due to be replaced by argon arc welding. The company was advised by these union officials and their members' representatives that each would strongly resist the concession to BMU of the latter's claim to a technique which was widely used by members of AC and EWU both locally and nationally.

    Both of these trade unions have consistently maintained this view and, despite the insistence by BMU that the current dispute concerns only the BMU and the company, it is the view of the company that any acceptable resolutions of the dispute will need to take into account the strongly held views of both AC and EWU and to be acceptable to these trade unions if further dispute is to be avoided.

    In submitting the dispute to arbitration the parties have agreed to seek assistance in resolving the issue. The difference between the parties concerns who should carry out this type of welding. The union argues that their exclusive rights to the work have already been established and should be continued. The company does not agree and maintains that argon arc welding has, in the past, been carried out on site by members of another union and that the use of the technique should not be considered the sole prerogative of any one trade union.

    (Signed)

    J. D. Sutton
    Works Director
    Smiths Chemicals Ltd

ASSOCIATED DOCUMENTS

Statement of agreement reached between Smiths Chemicals Ltd (the Company) and the Blacksmiths and Millwrights Union

The following is agreed as the basis for the return to work of blacksmiths employed by the company following the blacksmiths' strike with effect from 9 May.

1. The union maintains its claim that argon arc welding is a technique which should be the sole prerogative of members of their union and, specifically, that no argon arc welding should be carried out at Smiths Chemicals Ltd by coppersmiths or EWU workers.

2. The company maintains its claim that argon arc welding is a technique which can legitimately also be used at Smiths Chemicals by Coppersmiths and EWU workers and that the technique is not the sole prerogative of any single trade union.

3. Having hitherto failed to reach agreement on the above views, both parties agree to resolve the dispute by means of reference to an independent arbitrator to be appointed by the Advisory, Conciliation and Arbitration Service. The agreed terms of reference for the arbitrator are attached to this agreement.

4. To facilitate the resolution of the above dispute in a spirit of mutual trust and co-operation, it is agreed:

    (a) that no argon arc welding will be carried out on the company site by any outside contractor pending the outcome of arbitration;

    (b) that the company will defer the implementation of argon arc welding by the company's coppersmiths and EWU workers on breakdown, maintenance or capital work pending the outcome of arbitration. In the meantime, practical training of the company's coppersmiths will continue, but not on work associated with breakdown, maintenance or capital work;

    (c) that the blacksmiths will return to normal working with effect from 8.00 a.m. on 25 July.

Signed for the Blacksmiths and
Millwrights Union

....
District Official

....
Shop Steward

....
Date

Signed for Smiths Chemicals Ltd

....
Works Director

....
Personnel Services Manager

....
Date

Association of Coppersmiths

Guild House
15 Fraser Street
Bristol
10 May

K. Johnson, Esq.
14 Garforth Road
Bristol

Dear Ken

I thank you and acknowledge receipt of your letter indicating the training being offered to attempt to reach competency in argon arc welding.

The possible objections by the BMU should obviously be opposed by Smiths Chemicals on the grounds that no one trade has ever been given sole prerogative over welding and also that the use of argon arc is widely practised throughout industry by our membership, who merely accept it as one of the more proficient methods of welding.

Thank you for keeping me informed.

Yours faithfully,

ALAN NOAKES (signed)
District Secretary

Engineering Workers Union

United House
Portishead Avenue
Bristol

13 May

Mr J. D. Sutton
Smiths Chemicals Ltd
14 Portman Street
Bristol

Dear Mr Sutton

I understand from our shop steward that a dispute has arisen with the blacksmiths concerning objections they have to members of the Association of Coppersmiths and one of our own members undertaking argon arc welding. I trust that the dispute will be resolved satisfactorily but I do have to advise you that our members undertake argon arc welding all over this district and we would not readily concede this to be the sole work of one trade. Therefore, I trust that no work of this character be taken from our members without first discussing the matter in detail with myself.

Yours sincerely

W. SYKES (signed)
District Secretary

Association of Coppersmiths

Guild House
15 Fraser Street
Bristol

31 May

The arbitrator
Smiths Chemicals Ltd
14 Portman Street
Bristol

Dear Sir

Argon arc welding

I would firstly like to inform you that throughout the recent dispute pertaining to the introduction of argon welding, Mr Sutton has kept me fully conversant with all the relevant factors of this issue.

The situation relative to the coppersmith department is that we have not involved ourselves in any counter-claim to the BMU for the simple reason that it is our belief that to afford sole prerogative to any welding process to one trade is to beset future industry with problems that could be tantamount to disaster.

Our concern is that a welding process in the hands of one trade, irrespective of the type of work on which it is used, would be transferring complete control of industry from management to the custodian of the said process.

We are cognizant of the ludicrous situation which would prevail had the ratchet spanner or pump screwdriver been allocated to one set of workmen and we consider that this claim by BMU is in a similar vein.

You are no doubt aware that the argon welding is being used extensively in the sheet metal shops due to the cleanliness of the weld and we can quite understand the reason for its proposed introduction into the coppersmith and other trades work within Smiths Chemicals Ltd.

I have referred to the introduction of argon welding because, to date, the amount has been of such insignificance as to necessitate the usage of two and a half bottles of gas over a five year period.

Argon welding has, however, been used fairly extensively by contractors, especially 'Donovan' who employed the tradesmen most suitable to the work being undertaken, a practice which would have to be radically changed if the welding was the sole decider as to the type of trade being used.

As an association we have had lengthy talks with the EWU who, like ourselves, are of the opinion that a tradesman should be allowed to use modern methods on his own work and not have to rely, on every occasion, on the servicing by a second party when jointing is required.

The training and subsequent usage of argon welding is fairly commonplace within engineering and I can find no evidence of this training being used to usurp the normal function and customary field of work of another man's trade.

We sincerely hope that your findings in this dispute will not reverse the accepted practice of a man welding his own work within engineering maintenance and that you will quickly accept our fear of control from a servicing trade as justifiable and one affecting not only the coppersmith, but industry in general.

I thank you for this opportunity of putting in letter form some of the feelings of my members and I have for this reason declined from detailing shop practices in the various industries situated in Avon region.

Yours sincerely

A. NOAKES (signed)
District Secretary

Questions

1 Do you think that the company should have consulted with the black-smiths before embarking on the argon arc training for the coppersmiths?

2 Should the arbitrator accept the letter from Mr Noakes of the Copper-smith's Union when the dispute is between the blacksmiths and the company?

3 How would you resolve this issue?

Dispute between
PHOTOFILM LTD
and
the ASSOCIATION OF FILM PROCESSORS

**(concerning the grading of a number of jobs for
process workers)**

Background to the dispute

Photofilm Ltd operates at two sites, Hounslow in London and Chorlton in
Manchester. The Chorlton site is a manufacturing and distributing centre
for a wide range of photographic papers. Approximately 300 people are
employed on the site of whom 200 are process and general workers. The
jobs of these workers are graded according to a company-wide evaluation
scheme. This evaluation scheme was prepared by a joint management and
union team in 1982 and was revised in June 1986. It is the gradings of some
workers in the Coating Department at the Chorlton site which is the subject
of the present dispute.

In November last year, employee representatives from the Chorlton
Emulsion coating department requested a re-evaluation of all jobs in the
department. Because of difficulties in securing the services of two members
of the Central Job Evaluation Committee of the company, who are based
in Hounslow, these jobs were not evaluated until 10 July this year.

No upgradings resulted from these evaluations and a block appeal against
the results was registered. These appeals were heard on 18 July, but all of
them were turned down. The members of the coating department registered
a second appeal and a new and larger group from the Central Evaluation
Committee was set up to re-examine the job gradings in the coating
department.

As a result of this second appeal nine of the ten jobs were re-evaluated and
four of these were upgraded. The tenth job, that of the senior operator, was
not evaluated as its existing grade was the highest within the weekly paid
category. It was agreed that these upgradings would be back-dated to 1
January.

When these results were announced the members of the coating department took industrial action as a protest against what they saw as an unfair application of re-grading which eliminated a number of the traditional differentials between particular jobs. The men returned to work when the dispute was sent for an independent assessment.

Terms of reference

The suggested terms of reference for independent assessment are:

'To determine the correct grading of the jobs detailed below in the coating department within the context of the current job evaluation scheme and against the need to maintain a system of fair comparison with other jobs and to award accordingly.'

Jobs	Current grade
1. Reeler	III
2. Assistant reeler	II
3. Assistant coater	IV
4. Preparation operator	IA
5. Solutions dispenser	IB
6. Universal operator	SO(B)

UNION CASE

Association of Film Processors

Mr C.D. Horton   5a Lamb Lane
Personnel Manager   Denton
Photofilm Ltd   Manchester
Chorlton

Dear Sir

In November last year, all the employees in the coating department submitted a request for re-grading within the job evaluation scheme because they felt that changes in their work were not being taken account of, and re-gradings in other areas of the company were producing an imbalance in the relativities between themselves and other workers.

Two studies took place in July this year but no changes to the grades were required.

The members complained that incorrect information had been used. New job descriptions were issued for all the grades and a further study undertaken. This final study resulted in some jobs being re-graded and some remaining unchanged. The members in the re-graded jobs are satisfied with their results but the rest are not.

The highest graded job in the department is that of the universal operator who is paid senior operator Grade 'B' rate of pay and this job was not considered in the re-evaluation as the Company felt that whatever the results of the study this grade could not go any higher.

The members do not accept this and are of the opinion that the study should be carried out before a decision on this grade is arrived at. Should it be that a new grade is required within the scheme then one should be created, as was the case in 1984 (internal memo from C. D. Horton to E. A. Lawton, dated 23.8.84).

All the other jobs were re-evaluated using the job descriptions issued in August of this year. These descriptions are accepted by all concerned as accurate and correct.

However, as a result of a partial departmental re-grading, traditional and long accepted differentials have been destroyed. The stratification within the department had been accepted by everyone as fair and equitable, and the normal incentives were self-evident. This is no longer the case, and it is this basic alteration in the relativities which is the major reason for this request for arbitration.

Signed

P. JONES
Regional Organiser
Manchester Region

THE COMPANY CASE

Job Evaluation Grievance
Emulsion Coating Department

The Chorlton (Manchester) site of Photofilm Ltd is a manufacturing and distribution centre for a wide range of photographic papers and is one of the company's two major production units within the United Kingdom. The site employs 300 people, approximately 200 of whom are process and general workers whose job grades are determined by the evaluation scheme which is the subject of the grievance.

There are six recognised trade unions on the site, the largest being the Association of Film Processors (AFP) whose members are involved in the dispute.

There are 110 members of the AFP at Chorlton.

The existing job evaluation scheme for process and general workers has been in operation within this company for several years and was last amended in 1985 (copy attached as Appendix 1). It has been used to establish the grades for approximately 300 jobs within Photofilm Limited's UK manufacturing and distribution units.

Employee representatives from the emulsion coating department requested a re-evaluation of all jobs (10 in number) in January of this year. Due to difficulties in securing the services of the Central Job Evaluation Committee members, who are equally drawn from management and unions and who are based in London, the jobs were not evaluated until 10 July. The delay was caused by their commitment to the formulation of a new job evaluation scheme which is expected to supersede the existing scheme within the next few months.

The July evaluations were carried out by a committee consisting of:

- an independent chairman (from the central personnel department)
- two trades union representatives (from London)
- a convener – AFP – Chorlton
- a work study manager – Chorlton

In attendance, for the purpose of providing information, were:

- a manager – emulsion coating department
- chief shop steward – emulsion coating department

No upgradings resulted from the evaluations and a block appeal against the results was registered. The appeals were heard on 18 July but again, no upgradings resulted. A second appeal was registered. The evaluation committee was augmented by a work study officer from London and the Convener, AFP, from the Hounslow factory. Nine of the ten jobs were completely re-evaluated and four of the jobs were upgraded, the remaining five staying unchanged. The tenth job 'Senior Operator' was not evaluated as its existing grade is the highest within the weekly paid category. The effective date for the upgradings is 1 January.

The company contends that its job evaluation scheme for process and general workers, while not being ideal, attempts a comprehensive examination of job content. It has functioned in a generally satisfactory manner for several years on all UK sites. It has been operated on a joint management/union basis and has created a grading structure which has avoided the undesirable consequences of a structure based solely on management judgment. The evaluations which are the subject of the grievance were carried out under well established procedures by a joint management/union committee experienced in the workings of the scheme. Comprehensive job descriptions were used which had been agreed as being correct by union representatives. The workplace was visited by the committee and the jobs were seen in operation. Operators were questioned regarding the content of the job descriptions.

The company considers that the three evaluation sessions (including two appeals) described above represent one of the most exhaustive exercises ever carried out within Photofilm Limited. The company therefore believes that the gradings are correct and that the assessors should so find.

> C. D. Horton
> Personnel Manager
> Photofilm Ltd

Company Case (addendum)

The current job gradings are as follows:

Universal operator	SO(B)
Coater	SO(A)
Assistant coater	IV
2nd assistant coater	IV
Reeler	III
Assistant reeler	II
Melter	II
Preparation operator	IA
Solutions dispenser	IB
Relief assistants	

ASSOCIATED DOCUMENTS

Appendix 1

1 May 1982
(revised 22 June 1986)

Confidential
Photofilm Ltd Job Evaluation Scheme
for process personnel (excluding supervisors)

The number of points awarded to each factor must be based on the ability of the average trained person performing the job and also on the proportion of the time to which that factor applies.

It is important to remember that the **job** is being evaluated and not the person who does the job.

Factor   **Maximum**
                                                               score

1. **Complexity of instructions**   **32 points**
   Definition: the extent to which the job
                   demands the ability to
                   understand and put into effect
                   written orders or instructions.

(a) Occasional reference to simple orders/
    instructions (10 or less)   0–6

(b) Frequent reference to simple
    orders/instructions (10–20)   7–13

(c) Constant reference to simple orders/
    instructions (20+)

                   or   14–20

    Occasional reference to complex orders/
    instructions (10 or less)

Factor	**Maximum score**
(d) Frequent reference to complex orders/ instructions	21–26
(e) Constant reference to complex orders/ instructions	27–32

2. Alertness to detail   **20 points**
Definition: The extent to which alertness or concentration is required in order to perform the job well.

(a) Machine minding – automatic or reflex jobs (sweeping)	0–3
(b) Machine operating – jobs requiring ordinary visual attention	4–7
(c) Viewing (blemishes) – being very alert occasionally	8–11
(d) Work requiring close, continuous visual attention	12–15
(e) Detailed inspection – many variables (Control Room)	16–20

3. Complexity of task   **60 points**
Definition: the extent to which the job reflects the need to understand, memorise and implement details and variations.

(a) Doing the job in hand automatically – repetitive	0–12
(b) Routine work with little variation – not complex	13–24
(c) Variation in job – not complex	25–36

Factor		Maximum score

(d) Co-ordination required – variety within the job and some complexity   37–48

(e) Co-ordination of several activities at a time: both internal and external activities   49–60

4.   Dexterity   **20 points**
Definition: the extent to which the job requires the co-ordination between the muscles and the senses.

(a) Machine minding – little co-ordination   0–5

(b) Hand controlled – short cycle work, or where job efficiency depends on dextrous movements   6–12

(c) Extreme short cycle or intricate work   13–20

5.   Teamwork   **12 points**
Definition: the extent to which the co-operation is required between a number of people in the performance of the job.

Teamwork is either recognised in an established team or where the job demands contact and the exercise of discretion with others (excluding supervisors) in the normal execution of the job.

Either award one point for each member of an established team up to a maximum of 12 points

or

Award half a point for each necessary, regular contact with a maximum of six points.

Factor	Maximum score

6. Reasoning required 10 points

Definition: the extent to which judgment is required to perform the job and to recognise that the work is being done properly.

How much does the job require the operator to think? Can the process be performed easily or must the operator reason out the sequence of events?

(a) Routine repetitive work	0–2
(b) Work largely routine, but thought required	3–5
(c) Work no longer routine and thought required	6–8
(d) Considerable thought required	9–10

7. Materials 20 points

Definition: the extent to which one careless action can result in financial material loss.

Assess the value of that material and consider the proportion that would be lost. Calculate the cost of this proportion on the following basis:

	Value before silver recovery £	Value after silver recovery £
All emulsions per unit	15.00	5.00
All film products per sq metre	1.20	0.60
All paper products per sq metre	0.50	£ 0.40
All chemicals per litre	0.30	
One pallet of assorted products (ex chemicals)	1,500.00	
One pallet of chemicals	150.00	
One packed case	300.00	
One carton or package	50.00	

Factor				Maximum score

Score as below:

	0			12
£0–100	3	£1000–10 000		15
	6			18
	6			
£100–1000	9	Above		
		£10 000		20
	12			

8. Equipment   **4 points**

Definition: the extent to which carelessness may cause damage to equipment.

Award *one* point for each £175 worth of cost incurred in repair or replacement caused through lack of care, with a maximum of four points.

9. Subsequent operation   **16 points**

Definition: the extent to which carelessness affects later operations. Carelessness may cause additional work and it may have an adverse effect – not only on productions as a whole but also in distribution and on the customer.

	Level of responsibility
No effect on subsequent operations	0
Some effect on subsequent operations Little delay or cost	1–4

Factor	**Maximum Score**

Definite adverse effect on subsequent
operations and on cost (slight effect on
production)   5–8

Definite adverse effect on subsequent
operations, production as a whole –
re-work required   9–12

Serious effect on subsequent operations;
re-work affecting production as a
whole on other sites, depots, etc.   13–16

        Export packer = 8

Inspection can have an influence on this question. Where inspection can avert a disaster or partially avert, this should reduce the level of responsibility.

10. Darkroom environment   15 points
Allowance for darkroom work

In and out of darkroom (not subdued
white light) 10 or more times per
day/shift   5 points

No points to be scored for less than 10

11. Monotony   5 points
Definition: the extent to which the job
is tedious. Consider the
shortness of the cycle time
relative to the total time for
the batch work. Monotony
can also occur in long cycle
machine controlled
operations.

Intense and continual visual
attention to a limited variety
of work may result in
considerable monotony.

Award 0–5 points, according
to the degree of monotony.

Factor	Maximum score

12. Working position   **15 points**
   Definition: muscular strain involved in
            the normal performance of
            the job.

            Consider whether an unusual
            cramped position tends to
            strain certain muscles to an
            abnormal degree.

(a) Standing with little body movement   0–3

(b) Standing with no body movement or
    occasional stooping and reaching or
    standing and operating a foot pedal   4–6

(c) Frequent stooping and reaching   7–11

(d) Continual stooping and reaching   12–15

    Fork-lift driving (75%) = 2
    Baling   = 15

13. Physical effort   **30 points**
   Definition: the physical effort required
            to perform the job. The
            following table is intended
            as a guide:

    Work equivalent to:

(a) Lifting 9.072 kg (20lb) often
    or 22.680 kg (50lb) occasionally   0–9

(b) Lifting 22.680 kg (50lb) often
    or 45.360 kg (100 lb) occasionally   10–20

(c) Lifting 45.360 kg (100 lb) often
    or 79.379 kg (175 lb) occasionally   21–30

    Note: Occasionally means at least eight
          times during the working day

Factor   **Maximum**
                                                                    score

14. Working conditions   25 points

Definition: the extent to which the job
              requires working in non-
              standard conditions.

Examples:

Noise – press shop	6 points
Temperature – moulding machines	2 points
Noise – perforator room	9 points
Temperature and weather variations for people working predominantly outside	9 points
if, in addition, cold stores are frequented	12 points
Damp and fumes – solution-making in chemical packing	12 points
plus cold allowance	6 points
In and out of doors more than 10 times a day/shift	6 points
Fixer, chemical packing	4 points

15. Accident risk   25 points

Note: *any high risk score under the
         remaining factors must be
         reported to the safety officer
         immediately for action.*

Consider the chance of an accident happening and the possibility of that accident causing injury.

The severity of this injury should be assessed according to the following grading:

Low:	simple cuts or bruises
Medium:	serious cuts or a broken limb
High:	semi-permanent or permanent disablement

Factor		**Maximum score**

Points are now awarded to the following table:

Risk of injury	Severity of injury	Points
Nil	Nil	0
Low	Low	3
Low	Medium	9
Low	High	15
Medium	Low	6
Medium	Medium	12
Medium	High	20
High	Low	9
High	Medium	15
High	High	25

16.   Internal injury risk   15 points

Consider the risk of an internal injury such as hernia being caused by lifting or straining.

Working position and physical effort in the job should be reflected in this factor.

Low risk	0– 4
Medium risk	5– 9
High risk	10–15

17.   Disease risk   15 points

Consider the risk of contracting an industrial disease such as dermatitis.

Low risk	0– 4
Medium risk	5– 9
High risk	10–15

Jobs involving handling of coated materials score three points to recognise low risk (where gloves are not worn).

Point ranges per grade

0– 45	Grade IA
46– 70	Grade IB
71– 89	Grade II
90–120	Grade III
121–150	Grade IV
151–169	Grade SO (A)
170 upwards	Grade SO (B)

Appendix 2

Departmental job chart (Coating)

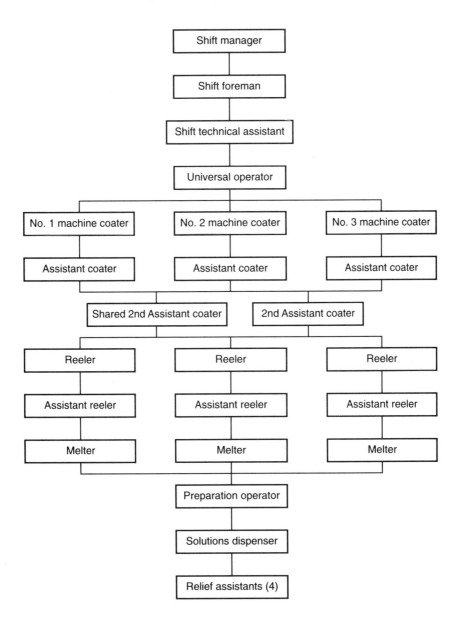

Comment and questions

In Appendix I the company's job evaluation scheme is set out in detail. In Appendix II the organisational structure chart for the coating department is given. These are company documents but are not in contention.

In addition to the written evidence submitted, a number of points have been made by union officials and the shop stewards to the officers preparing the case. Similarly there is supplementary material from the management side. These comments are set out below.

The union points out that during the past five years there have been changes in work context and practices, new machines have been introduced and different chemical mixes are now used. All of this has resulted in a much greater throughput of photofilm than before which has resulted in the operators working harder and carrying much more responsibility.

Other departments have been regraded to reflect these changes and the staff at the coating department were surprised and disappointed when the regrading exercise resulted in no upgrading at all. They point out that the operatives felt cheated and were pleased when job descriptions were re-assessed. It has been doubly disappointing that only four jobs were re-graded as a result and they warn that the resulting tensions caused by the new anomalies in differentials is producing disaffection which will lead to unavoidable industrial action.

The company points out that the job evaluation scheme works well and that there have been no complaints from the other plants. In response to requests a second evaluation was conducted and they state that this was done extremely thoroughly by a national team of equal representatives from union and management.

In addition the company states that the re-gradings in other departments took place because there were job losses and amalgamations when new machinery was introduced but these changes did not affect the coating department.

Also, in the coating department the overall productivity is much as before and there have been no significant cost savings. This makes it impossible for the company to afford unjustified re-gradings.

The assessors should take all factors into account in reaching their decision but may make recommendations as they see fit.

1   Does the job evaluation scheme contain too large band widths for the jobs and structure in the department?

2   Does the evaluation scheme concentrate too much on the physical aspects of jobs rather than planning, co-ordinating and responsibility aspects?

3   Are there other ways of establishing appropriate differentials than creating a series of new grades?

Dispute between
SLADE RUBBER LTD
and
the UNION OF RUBBER MACHINE
OPERATORS

(concerning the payment of team allowance to the leading hand of the group working with cutting machines)

Terms of reference

The terms of reference agreed by both parties are:

'To determine whether team allowance should be paid to the strip cutter operators in the rubberised fabric section at Slade Rubber Ltd, Salford.'

Background to the dispute

Slade Rubber Ltd is a composite factory employing workers in two separate divisions. These are tyre manufacture and belting. These divisions are autonomous and have differences in their management structure. Each management group is responsible to the general manager of the respective division and each division has considerable latitude in respect of marketing, financial management and policy making.

The tyre division consists of five departments operating on a three shift, five working days system. Depending upon its size and function each department has a number of sections each of which is responsible for one or more operations in the stages of manufacture. Certain operations can only be accomplished by a group of people and it is possible for a section to have a number of such group operations of different sizes within it.

There is a considerable history of joint negotiations and agreement between the tyre division and the Union of Rubber Machine Operators going back many years. One of these agreements relates to team allowance, the area of the present union claim.

The management of the tyre division and the local officials of the Union of Rubber Machine Operators reached agreement many years ago that three or more people in a group operation constituted a team. It was further agreed that a monetary allowance known as a team allowance would be paid to one particular operator within such teams. Although the original agreement is unavailable there appears to be no dispute as to the details. Following a union claim several years ago these arrangements were re-negotiated and a document was published giving details of the new agreement. While mentioning the amounts to be paid as a responsibility or team allowance to leading hands in a team, this document does not state the minimum number of people constituting a team.

The shop members of the Union of Rubber Machine Operators put forward a claim two years ago for a team allowance to be paid to the operators of strip cutter machines. A number of other points were put forward at that time and the request for a team allowance was not progressed. A further meeting was held on 24 June last year when a specific claim for team allowance for the leading hand on strip cutter machines was put forward by the union and it is this unresolved claim which has been referred to arbitration with the agreement of both parties in May of this year.

LETTER FROM THE UNION TO THE ARBITRATOR

Union of Rubber Machine Operators

Unity House
Paradise Road
Salford

To: the independent arbitrator

Dear Sir

Terms of reference

'To determine whether team allowance should be paid to the strip cutter operators in the rubberised fabric section at Slade Rubber, Salford.'

The claim is in respect of four men who each control a two man team. From time to time during the shift they also control three, four or even five men. Claim submitted in 1978.

A team allowance of 2.5p per hour is paid at the moment for control of a team as per original agreement (*see* Appendix 1 and 2. Associated documents).

Points in support

The job originally was a three man team and, in the main, manually operated. It is now, in the main, automatic and a two man team with the same output and control.

The operator is in sole charge of the job and the operator would not have it any other way. Unless properly controlled it could be extremely dangerous with running nips, revolving knives, etc.

The team is increased from time to time and they then come under control of an operator, i.e. stacker driver, boardmen (2), leading hand and other operators as required.

A team allowance is paid for two man teams in other areas of the Salford site.

> BILL BAKER
> Convenor – URMO
>
> Slade Rubber Ltd
> Tyre Division
> Salford

COMPANY CASE TO ARBITRATOR

Slade Rubber Ltd – Salford

Management case for arbitration enquiry on dispute between Slade Rubber Ltd, tyre division, and the Union of Rubber Machine Operators.

Agreed terms of reference

'To determine whether team allowance should be paid to the strip cutter operator in the rubberised fabric section at Slade Rubber Limited, Salford.'

Background

The Slade Rubber establishment at Salford is a composite factory employing workers in two separate divisions, manufacturing tyres and belting. The multi-divisional organisation has carried with it a diversification in management structure. The two autonomous management groups are responsible to the general manager of their respective divisions and there are widely differing considerations in respect of, for example, marketing, financial systems, budgetary controls and policy making.

Tyre division operations

The tyre division consists of five departments operating on a three shift, five days working, namely:

1. rubber compound and fabric preparation
2. crossply tyre manufacture
3. radial tyre manufacture
4. inspection and repairs
5. storage and despatch

Dependent upon the size and function, each department has a number of sections each of which is responsible for one or more operations in the stages of manufacture. Certain operations can only be done by a group of people and it is possible for a section to have a number of such group operations all varying in size.

History of team allowance

The tyre division management and the local officials of the URMO reached agreement many years ago that three or more people in a group operation constituted a team and for a monetary allowance, henceforth known as a team allowance, to be paid to one particular operator within each team. The original agreement is no longer to hand but following a claim from the trade union the following was agreed. Such operators became known as working leading hands and accepted responsibility for co-ordinating the activities of the group together with ensuring that production and quality targets were met. The team allowance, which is in addition to the job rate, varies in accordance with the number of people employed within the team, viz:

No. of operators in team (including leading hand)	Pence per hour
3 or 4	2.5
5 to 7 (inclusive)	3.0
8 to 11 (inclusive)	3.5

Union of Rubber Machine Operators

The URMO which represents all the process workers and has the sole negotiating rights for the site, submitted a specific claim two years ago for a team allowance to be paid to one man out of a two man crew employed on the strip cutter machines in the crossply tyre rubberised fabric section. The operation of the strip cutter entails cutting rolls of rubberised fabric into strips which, in a subsequent operation, go to form the carcass of a motor tyre. There are two such machines, one operates on a three shift system and one is worked on day shift only. There are, therefore, four two man crews and the total claim would involve four people. This operation, until approximately 10 years ago, required a three man crew but with the introduction of an electronic sensing device the number was reduced to two by agreement with the trade union.

The trade union claims that a factory agreement exists which specifies an allowance for a two man team. They take the view also that responsibility for work being done is the same whether a team is two or three and when more than one person is involved in an operation a team allowance is justified.

Management view

Tyre division management takes the view that responsibility and skills attached to any job are recognised in the job rate and are always taken into consideration when a job rate is being negotiated. A team allowance, on the other hand, is paid for having responsibility for more than one person and this is precisely the criterion on which the original agreement was based. Further to that the agreement was reviewed several years ago by tyre division management and the trade union and the terms as a result are very specific in relation to the constitution of a team.

Tyre division management is aware that following the review, a claim was made for a similar agreement to operate within the belting division. Following a meeting between belting division management and shop stewards an agreement was reached which in every respect was similar to that in the tyre division. Since that time, it would appear that the agreement in the belting division has been wrongly interpreted and payments have been awarded quite erroneously. This is a matter for the belting division to put right and does not, in any way, change the agreement for the tyre division.

Conclusion

Both parties have discussed the issue at every stage of the procedure for dealing with requests and complaints (minutes attached) and the procedure has now been exhausted. By agreement, the matter has been passed to arbitration and tyre division management will abide by the decision of the arbitrator.

Signed

F. C. Thomson
Production Manager

ASSOCIATED DOCUMENTS

Slade Rubber Ltd – Belting Division
Stage 4A of Procedure
Substantial increase leading operators
Meeting held in the conference room at 12.15 p.m.
13 April 1975

Present:

Mr J. White – Chairman

Management members:	Shop representatives:
Mr D. Allison	Mr S. Prince
Mr K. Roberts	Mr A. G. Roberts
Mr J. A. Snead	Mr J. Taylor – URMO
Mr S. Vaughan	
Mr T. Vale	

Mr Taylor said that this is a claim for an increase for leading hands on the calenders and extruders and by the notes has been thoroughly discussed at previous stages. He would suggest that there is no necessity to go through all the details again and in order to effect a speedy solution if possible, would suggest a basis for settlement, but at the same time indicate that there was little or no room for compromise in this proposal. It is considered that there should be two groupings with appropriate enhancement of the leading hands payment as follows:

'Y' box extruder	⎫	to 4p per hour
'O' line extruder		
Car extruder	⎬	
No. 12 Calender		
No. 11 Calender	⎭	to 3p per hour
No. 13 Calender		

Mr S. Prince said that it is considered that this is a reasonable expectation with a two grouping system or three groups at the very most.

Meeting adjourned at 12.25 p.m. and resumed at 12.35 p.m.

The chairman said that after consideration management is prepared to move to meet this proposal, but not quite to the terms suggested. It is prepared as a settlement to offer the following groupings and appropriate payment for leading hands:

'Y' box extruder	to 3.5p per hour
'O' line extruder	to 3p per hour
Car extruder	
No. 12 calender	
No. 11 calender	to 2.5p per hour
No. 13 calender	

Meeting adjourned at 12.40 p.m. and resumed at 12.45 p.m.

Mr Taylor said that after consideration management's proposal would be acceptable as a settlement of this claim. He then requested retrospective payment.

The chairman agreed this payment.

Mr S. Prince said that it would be as well to show in the agreement that the retrospective payment would apply to all hours worked since the starting date. This would obviate problems and excess payments.

The Chairman agreed.

Meeting closed at 12.50 p.m.

Appendix 1

Slade Rubber – Belting Division
Substantial increase leading hands

At a meeting held at Stage 4A of procedure on 13 April 1975 the following was agreed:

1. It was agreed to introduce three groupings for the calenders and extruders for payment purposes to leading hands. The appropriate payment to each grouping leading hand as follows:
    (a) 'Y' box extruder   3.5p
    (b) 'O' line extruder   3p
         Car extruder
    (c) No. 12 calender
         No. 11 calender   2.5p
         No. 13 calender
         Chafer buffing
2. Retrospective payment of the difference between these payments and old payments for all hours worked from 10 August 1974.

.... Chairman
.... District Organiser, URMO
.... Shop Representatives' Secretary
.... Shop Representative

Appendix 2

Slade Rubber Ltd – Belting Division
Team allowance

At a stage 6A meeting with the shop representatives on 22 June 1975 the following was agreed:

Up to a total team of 4 operators	2.50p per hour
Up to a total team of 7 operators	3.00p per hour
Up to a total team of 11 operators	3.50p per hour

Effective 20 June 1975
Retrospective 10 August 1974

Signed:

Personnel	Production	Shop	Shop
Manager	Manager	Representative	Representative

Attachment 1

Crossply Tyre Department

Management request

February 1977

Section Rubberised fabric

Request For a team allowance for leading operators (4) on strip cutters, rubberised fabric section.

Reason for request Responsibility

Departmental manager's comments

The department manager does not consider that a team allowance should be paid because the responsibility involved does not compare with that of running a high level banner.

As no agreement could be reached the case was passed to Stage 4 of the procedure.

.... Shop Representative

.... Shop Representative

.... Shop Representative

.... Departmental Manager

Attachment 2

Tyre Division

Shop request – rubberworks

Stage 4 of Procedure

Meeting held in the conference room at 12.15 p.m. on 20 June 1977

For team allowance for leading operator (4) on strip cutters – rubberised fabric section

Present:

Mr J. F. Nixon – Chairman

Management members:
Mr P. Owen
Mr A. R. Hollis

Shop representatives:
Mr S. Pemberton
Mr B. Baker
Mr B. A. Bassett
Mr R. Callon

The chairman read the request and the comments made at Stage 3.

Mr Pemberton said the terms of reference had been put in on his recommendation. He said he was not attempting to make comparisons of the strip cutters to the other cutters but that teams of two men and upwards should be paid a minimum team allowance.

Mr Owen said the strip cutter team was only two men, the cutter driver was paid the B rate because he was the senior man.

Mr Pemberton said that every team had differentials because of the difference in skill content but there should also be a team allowance.

Mr Owen replied the driver did not control any other operator.

Mr Baker said the driver did control the activities of the other man. He said the job had been at one time a three-man team, sometimes a four-man team. He considered one man was responsible for the job and for what the other man did.

Mr Pemberton said Mr Baker had stated that if one man was responsible, he asked who would decide when the machine was stopped or started. Mr Pemberton said that when there was a problem, management would state who should be in charge and he made reference to an occasion in the belting factory when a serious breakdown had occurred, the blame had been laid against an operator who management had said was in charge. Mr Pemberton said B Grade payment was made for special skills.

Mr Owen said the representatives made the job sound more complicated than it actually was. The cutter driver did not manage any other people who had to do work involving a technical skill and he asked the question 'how far do we go to in the delegation of work'.

Mr Pemberton said they would consider withdrawing the request and re-phrasing it as a four-man team job.

Mr Owen said it was definitely only a two-man job.

Meeting adjourned at 12.30 p.m. and resumed at 12.45 p.m.

The chairman said there were no agreements relating to two-man team jobs receiving team allowance. He said management considers there should only be a difference in the grade allowance.

Mr Pemberton said he considered there was a degree of responsibility in a two-man team job dealing with machinery of that nature. He would register a failure to agree and move the request to the next stage of procedure.

Meeting closed at 12.52 p.m.

Any agreements or commitments contained in these minutes are not legally enforceable and are binding in honour only.

June 1977

Attachment 3

Tyre Division

Shop request – rubberworks

Stage 5 of Procedure

Meeting held in the works council chamber at 11.35 a.m. on 24 October 1977

For team allowance for leading operators (4) on strip cutters – rubberised fabric section

Present:

Mr B. Forest – Chairman

Management members:	Shop representatives:
Mr F. C. Thomson	Mr J. B. Hague
Mr J. F. Nixon	Mr E. J. Riley
Mr J. R. English	Mr B. Baker
Mr J. Pemberton	Mr S. Dunn
Mr A. S. Shepperd	Mr K. W. Metcalf
	Mr A. Crawley

Mr Hague said the claim was in respect of four men. They each controlled a team of two men inclusive of themselves and he believed there was already a factory agreement in existence that justified the claim. Mr Hague said the team strength had been three men but with the introduction of a magic eye the team had been reduced to two men. There were times, however, when difficulties were experienced with the fabric and the team was increased to three or four men. Mr Hague said that at the Stage 4 meeting management claimed it was only a two man job and that the job was not as complicated as the representatives had suggested. The representatives had claimed there was already agreement on site for team allowances for two man teams and had asked management to check that fact. A failure to agree had been registered. Mr Hague said he had established there were agreements in the belting factory for a team allowance to be paid to a team of two men, e.g. the dipper unit, the lining machine and also on eight presses.

Mr Thomson said that the cutter driver did not control the stacker driver: the stacker driver had contact because of the nature of the job but he was not part of the team.

Mr Baker said the cutter driver had to give instructions to a certain extent, but the claim was based on when only one man was controlled. It was realised there were agreements for teams of three and upwards but this was a two man team which could at times be five men.

Mr Thomson said the abnormalities should not be considered with the claim. If and when there were abnormalities management took special action.

The chairman said the stacker driver and other people should be disregarded. The claim put forward by the representatives was based on the responsibility of the job and that there were agreements elsewhere.

Mr Thomson asked was the request being used as a basis for establishing two men team jobs.

Mr Hague said he was only discussing a specific machine.

The chairman said the machine should be discussed in isolation.

Mr Nixon said he did not believe there was a written agreement for a two man team.

The chairman said any such agreement should not be used as the basis of an argument.

Mr Metcalf said the responsibility of a strip cutter really qualified for a team allowance.

Mr Baker said it was a very responsible job and it also controlled other people's work.

Mr Thomson said he was surprised that such a fundamental point was being used as a platform for the claim. He said the team was originally three, but when it had been reduced to two men the pay rate had also been adjusted.

Mr Baker said that when it had been a three man job no team allowance had been paid, but the representatives felt that it was an appropriate time to ask for an allowance.

Mr Hague said that when the agreement was negotiated for a reduction to a two man team an allowance was given for a B Grade man.

Mr Thomson said the discussion emphasised the need for a set of rules by which the factory should work. Management could only point out that within the tyre factory there was no agreement where a team allowance was paid in respect of a group of two men.

Mr Shepherd read the agreement regarding leading hand payments made at Stage 6B of procedure.

Mr Hague said the point made was that the more men you were responsible for the more money you should receive, there should be a value placed against responsibility.

The chairman asked what were the grades when it had been a three man team.

Mr Baker said 1 MB and 2 MA.

Mr Thomson said that when the driver's job was replaced by the use of a magic eye, one man was made MB grade and the other MA grade.

Mr Baker said the MB man had many controls to operate and that on a similar machine employing three men there was a team allowance.

Mr J. Pemberton asked did the three man team job mentioned by Mr Baker receive the same rates of pay as did the job under discussion.

Mr Baker replied the pay rates were different but it was not rates of pay that were being discussed.

Mr Riley asked that if a team allowance payment was made, was it necessary to have a number of different grades in that team job.

Mr Shepherd said it was not necessary.

Meeting adjourned at 11.55 a.m. and resumed at 12.18 p.m.

The chairman said that after consideration management considered that a claim for a team of only two men was not justified. He said that if new terms of reference were put in concerning the grade of the job, then the job could be re-examined and the work content re-assessed.

Mr Crawley asked was the pattern of future negotiation to be based on the re-studies of jobs.

The chairman said that decisions made should be done on a professional basis. Decision should not be reached by a yes, no or maybe attitude; requests should not be prejudged and each should be judged on its merits. The chairman said he would like a complete job evaluation to be carried out but this would be a long term solution.

Mr Crawley asked did the chairman mean every case would have to be re-studied.

The chairman replied no, only the jobs that necessitated a study.

Mr Baker asked the chairman was he suggesting that new terms of reference should be submitted.

The chairman replied yes, so that the job could be re-valued, jobs had to be looked at relative to other jobs.

Mr Thomson said that by doing a work study or by joint involvement of a committee to carry out job evaluation, a set of figures can be produced which set out jobs in the relative values.

Mr Hague said he was not interested in a lecture on job evaluation, if it was necessary to carry out a study concerned with a request procedure, the study should be done before Stage 5.

Mr Metcalf said the procedure system was not intended to revert from Stage 5 to Stage 3; the workers side of the committee may have to consider whether in future the procedure system should be used in their negotiation.

The chairman said he was not suggesting that the request should go back in procedure, but that further terms of reference be submitted.

Mr Crawley said the point had been made by Mr Parker at a previous meeting, other factories had accepted the introduction of new techniques of work measurement, but had received a lead in pay. He said Salford would not accept any new routines.

Mr Baker said there was no necessity to re-study the strip cutter job, its work content was already well known.

Mr Hagan said he would register a failure to agree and move to the next stage of procedure.

Meeting closed at 12.30 p.m.

Attachment 5

Tyre Division

Shop request – rubberworks

Stage 6A of Procedure

Meeting held in the works conference room at 10.15 a.m. on 16 December 1978

For team allowance for leading operators (4) on strip cutters – rubberised fabric section

Present:

Mr B. Forest – Chairman

Management members: Shop representatives:
Mr F. C. Thomson   Mr B. Arnold
Mr A. S. Shepherd   Mr J. B. Hague
Mr J. F. Nixon   Mr B. Baker
Mr A. R. Victor   Mr R. Carter
                             Mr B. Bassett

Mr Baker said the claim was in respect of four men each of whom controlled a two man team. Originally the team strength had been three men but with the introduction of modern techniques, the team had been reduced to two men. Although the work done by the two men was the same as that done by the three man team, at no time had additional cash been awarded in respect of labour savings. The cutter driver had to control the work of two servicemen, give instructions to the stacker driver and when material difficulties were experienced the team could be increased to three, four or even five men.

The chairman said he did not believe that the spasmodic control over the serviceman should be considered as being part of a team function. When a third, fourth and fifth person had to be used in addition to the two man team, the leading hand allowance would be paid. Management could not pay the allowance for less than a three man team.

Mr Baker said the cutter operator controlled the same amount of work being done by two men as was done by three men, he therefore had the same responsibility.

The chairman said the leading hand allowance was for the responsibility of people.

Mr Thomson said the cutter driver had no responsibility over the servicemen and the contact with the stacker driver was only because of the nature of the work.

Mr Hague said the operator still had the responsibility to see that the job was set up correctly.

Mr Arnold said the basic difference was that the union side considered two men constituted a team but management stipulated it was a minimum of three.

The chairman said there was an agreed payment scale for a team of three or more men. On the specific job under discussion, two men did not qualify for a team allowance but a differential payment was made.

Mr Baker said that management had conceded that the team strength could increase: that two men did the same work as was previously carried out by three men and added that the cutter driver's operations now consisted of pressing buttons rather than turning wheels. A team allowance had only recently (1975) been established for three men and the representatives were attempting to establish an allowance for two men.

Mr Thomson said the allowance was paid on those occasions when the team strength increased above two men and that as machinery became more sophisticated it was sometimes necessary to change the method of operation. People therefore would have to work at times in pairs and nobody directed the activities of two man teams.

Mr Baker said that if a five man team was reduced to four men he believed the team allowance would be negotiated accordingly. The responsibility of the three man team had remained with the cutter driver when the team had reduced to two men, by the same principle of a five to four reduction, a team allowance should be negotiated when reducing from a three to a two man team.

The chairman said that on the hypothetical case suggested he believed rates would be re-negotiated when team strengths were altered.

Mr Baker said that in a three man team when there was absenteeism the team allowance would still be paid.

Mr Nixon said that would be because the circumstances would only be of a temporary nature.

Meeting adjourned at 10.45 a.m. and resumed at 11.00 a.m.

Mr Arnold said there was no point in going around in circles. It was accepted that management did not agree to a team being of only two men;

the representatives considered it was a team when more than one person was involved in an operation and an allowance was justified.

A failure to agree was registered and the request was moved to Stage 6B.

Meeting closed at 11.05 a.m.

Attachment 6

Shop request – rubberworks

Stage 6B of Procedure (rubberised fabric)

For team allowance (leading hand, for strip cutters)

Meeting held on Friday 24 June last year in the works conference room

Present:

Mr M. Keenan – Chairman

Management members:	Shop representatives:
Mr B. Forest	Mr P. Miller
Mr F. C. Thomson	Mr B. Arnold
Mr J. Brazier	Mr B. Baker
Mr A. R. Victor	Mr W. Parker
Mr J. F. Nixon	Mr B. Bassett

Mr Baker said the claim was for four strip cutter operators who controlled teams of two men. At the present time the tyre division only paid team allowance when there was a minimum of three men involved, but it was the representatives' contention that although the two men of the team were paid at the MA and MB rates of pay the cutter driver had indirect control over three men, i.e. the stacker driver and two ply board men. It was also a fact that when material difficulties arose the team could be increased by three, four or even five men. Originally the operation had been a three man team job but, because of technological progress, had been reduced to two.

Mr Keenan questioned the involvement of the indirect control. In reply, Mr Baker said the cutter driver had to give instructions throughout his shift and, although management claimed it was the foreman who gave the instructions, this was not the case.

Mr Miller said the same amount of work was being done as previously, therefore the responsibility for work done was the same and it could be claimed the responsibility for work was greater than that associated with numbers of people. The trend in the industry was that as machinery became more sophisticated the labour force was reduced. Therefore, although efficiency could increase, the claim for team allowance could disappear. Mr Miller asked where the line could be drawn between direct and indirect control. He considered the situation should be reviewed and a sliding scale applied according to the numbers being 'looked after'.

Mr Parker made the point that the team could be increased at any time and could even become as large as eight men. A person with responsibility of such a nature should not just be Grade 'B'; in the old days he would have been at least Grade 'C'. It was the first time he had learnt anywhere that as a result of increased efficiency, a rate of pay had not increased. There were anomalies in the plant, as in the belting factory, where team allowance was paid when there were only two men in a team.

The meeting adjourned 2.05 p.m.

The meeting resumed 2.30 p.m.

Mr Keenan said he was not prepared to take the anomalies into account; agreements were peculiar to individual factories. There was already a planner and a leading hand in that area who made known the requirements of the foreman to the people involved in the operation. A team allowance was made for looking after people but the 'team' claimed by the union side was only the exchange of words which developed and built up between groups of workers. He said he sympathised with the remarks concerning changing skills and technology but said that was a much broader issue. He therefore could not agree to the claim. Mr Keenan said the wage structure had built up historically on a piecemeal basis and management now considered that the total field of general responsibilities should be investigated.

Mr Miller said that a categorical 'no' from the company generally led to a failure to agree. He suggested it might be preferable to stand the meeting adjourned pending the review of the whole wage structure. Mr Parker said that the reply by the company indicated that it did not recognise the additional duties done by the cutter driver and he said that the duties could be stopped. Mr Thomson said he considered the operation would still be able to function.

Mr Keenan said the union side was entitled to put its request into procedure but he did not consider it was a valid one. The time would seem opportune to look at the whole wage structure. Mr Parker said that management had exploited the increase in efficiency by penalising people by not paying them team allowance.

Mr Bassett said that management had indicated the operation could function even if the cutter driver stopped carrying out extra duties and he questioned the problems that could arise if people were not directed to assist when there were material difficulties. Mr Keenan said such occasions were only of a temporary nature.

Mr Thomson outlined the duties performed by the planner and leading hand. Mr Baker said that if it was left to the two people mentioned, the job would never get off the ground, he emphasised that it was the cutter driver who became directly involved with the whole operation. Mr Parker said he understood it was a policy of the company that a person should not be worse off because of increased efficiency. Mr Thomas pointed out that the work involved had been a specific laid down operation but people had tended to develop their own system.

Mr Bassett said that if team allowance was not paid when additional men were brought in to assist, the work would stop. Mr Keenan said he would be prepared to look at that set of circumstances. Mr Miller reaffirmed his view that team allowance should be paid when additional men were used and he could not understand why the company were disregarding payment for a team allowance for two men when it was already operating on the site.

The meeting adjourned 3.15 p.m.

The meeting resumed 3.30 p.m.

Mr Keenan said the company would agree to pay team allowance when the team was increased by one or more operators at the direction of the foreman. Mr Hiller said the union side would accept the company offer but he would remind management that the cutter crew would only be working to their job descriptions and that problems could arise; the problems would be the concern of the management. Team allowance was paid in other parts of the factory when there were only two men in the team. He could not accept that an employer should treat employees differently in various sections in the factory – this was a wrong approach by the company and the matter should be referred to ACAS.

The meeting adjourned 3.40 p.m.

The meeting resumed 3.45 p.m.

Mr Keenan said he was prepared, on behalf of the company, for the matter to be referred to ACAS. He would assume that as arbitration was a continuation of the procedure, no action would be taken by the union side. Mr Miller said the terms of reference to be submitted to ACAS would be: 'To determine whether team allowance should be paid to the strip cutter operator in the rubberised fabric section at Slade Rubber Ltd, Salford'.

Mr Miller asked whether it would be difficult to monitor every occasion when team allowance would be paid. In reply, Mr Keenan said that he could see difficulties but if the findings of ACAS were in favour of the union, the situation of monitoring each occasion would only last for a short while.

The meeting closed 4.00 p.m.

Attachment 7

Tyre Division Agreement

Rubberised fabric section

Fork lift stacker driver

The following was agreed at Stage 3 of procedure 22.7.77:

1. That the stacker driver would remove any part-rolls to and from the cutters as and when necessary, using metal extension channels and store on lower fabric storage racks only, moving aside as and when necessary to obtain full rolls of fabric.
2. That for this additional work the stacker drivers would receive £3/week each (2.66 p/hr) paid as a plus payment until such time as an automatic wind-back device is fitted to the machine and in working order, at which time the payment would cease.
3. While no guarantee can be given as to when the automatic re-wind will be in operation on the machine, every effort will be made to have it fitted as soon as possible.
4. Date of implementation of operation and payment 26.6.77.

.... Shop Representative
.... Shop Representative
.... Shop Representative
.... Departmental Manager

Operation time and instruction sheet

Operation   Cutting fabric pieces on electronic cutter   Sheet no. 1
                no. 1 and no. 2 cutters   Record no. 0381

Item no.	Sub-operations to be performed to fulfil piecework conditions	*Time allowance (minutes)*
1.	Machine cut fabric	0.0820
2.	Change bias angle (basic minutes per occasion = 0.305)	
	1 occasion per 67 cuts	0.0046
3.	Change machine to cut different width (basic minutes per occasion = 0.242)	
	1 occasion per 35 cuts	0.0068
4.	Mark up on fabric using rubber crayon, details, size, etc. (basic minutes per occasion = 0.263)	
	1 occasion per 35 cuts	0.0082
5.	Piece of fabric aside after changing bias angle (basic minutes per occasion = 0.195)	
	1 occasion per 67 cuts	0.0030
6.	Check size after changing width, using measuring rule (basic minutes per occasion = 0.154)	
	1 occasion per 35 cuts	0.0044
7.	Check dockets for size, quantity and bias angle, etc. (basic minutes per occasion = 0.297)	
	1 occasion per 47 cuts	0.0063
8.	Change plyboards (full one aside, empty board in position) (basic minutes per occasion = 0.256)	
	1 occasion per 35 cuts	0.0073
9.	Adjust knife in cutting machine using stone (basic minutes per occasion = 1.02) (includes change, sharpen, reset as necessary)	
	1 occasion per 557 cuts	0.0019
10.	Walk to end of roll to check on material on roll (basic minutes per occasion = 0.298)	
	1 occasion per 140 cuts	0.0021
	Total	0.1266
	5% contingency allowance	0.0063
	Total	0.1329
	1/19th personal allowance	0.0070
	Standard time for 1 fabric cut =	0.1399

Effective date: 3.4.67

Operation time and instruction sheet

Operation Rubberised fabric, ply board servicing Sheet no. 1
no. 1 and no. 2 cutters using ply board Record no. 0417
truck and ply boards

Item no. Sub-operations to be performed to fulfil *Time*
piecework conditions *allowance*
(minutes)

Description: travel with cut fabric from cutters to binding
tables with truck and ply board loaded carrying
on average 40 fabric pieces per journey.

1.	Load full board	0.102
2.	Travel with loaded board to destination	0.235
3.	Manoeuvre at location (basic minutes per occasion = 0.171)	
	1 occasion per 2 journeys (approx.)	0.0734
4.	Unload full board	0.114
5.	Transfer cut pieces on part loaded board (basic minutes per occasion = 0.180)	
	1 occasion in 3 journeys (approx.)	0.058
6.	Transfer full board 'bottom to top' ready for binders (basic minutes per occasion = 0.210)	
	1 occasion in 3 journeys (approx.)	0.095
7.	Load empty board to truck (basic minutes per occasion = 0.119)	
	1 occasion in 2 journeys (approx.)	0.062
8.	Travel with empty board on truck, or unladen truck to cutters	0.231
9.	Unload empty board (basic minutes per occasion = 0.102)	
	1 occasion in 2 journeys	0.053
10.	Decide destination of materials (basic minutes per occasion = 0.387)	
	1 occasion in 12 journeys (approx.)	0.033
11.	Instructions foreman, planner and leading hand (basic minutes per occasion = 0.271)	
	1 occasion in 20 journeys (approx.)	0.013
	Total	1.069
	5% contingency allowance	0.053
	Total	1.122
	1/19th personal allowance	0.0059
	Total standard minutes per 40 fabric pieces per journey	1.181

Note: the above values include allowances for taking full boards to stock
areas and taking full boards from stock areas to binding tables.

Job break-down sheet for training worker in new operation

Part Cutter   **Operation** Cutting

Important steps in the operation	Key points
Step: a logical segment of the operation which substantially advances the work.	*Key point*: anything in step that might: make or scrap the work; injure the worker; make the work easier to do; i.e. 'knack', 'trick', special timing, bit of information
1. Operate switch to 'on' position	Knife pitted correctly
2. Press 'start' button. Rotate bias angle at bridge assembly to read bias	Check knife control is on 'hand'. Correct bias
3. Adjust rule to correct width	Rule control switch on bridge assembly
4. Trim bias angle	Keep material to minimum. Hand switch on bridge assembly
5. Set speed selector to desired speed	Low for any size under 24 in.
6. Press button for moving conveyor forward	Keep hand off conveyor
7. Change knife switch to 'auto'. Bring fabric forward by inch button	Inch button on right of panel
8. Operate knife control to forward	Keep hand off conveyor

Compiled by ....

Questions

1 Do you think the strip cutter operators who already earn more than their colleagues on the machines should receive a further payment for managing a team of one other person?
2 What is your opinion of the way in which the procedure meetings were conducted?
3 What is the relevance of the job description of the fork lift stacker driver?

Arbitration between
RIVERSIDE BREWING LTD
and
the UNION BREWERY EMPLOYEES

**(in respect of the application of a productivity scheme to
certain delivery men)**

Terms of reference

The terms of reference agreed by both parties were:

> 'To consider the union's claim that the barrel delivery fleet was
> unreasonably excluded from the company productivity scheme until
> 1 January this year on the grounds of declining to agree a statement of
> intent concerning self-financing productivity savings, this not being a
> condition applicable to all sections of employees covered by the scheme,
> and to award accordingly.'

Documentation

The arbitrator received a full statement of the case from Riverside Brewing
Limited. In addition he was provided with documents describing the
productivity agreements and procedures within the company. He also
received a submission from the Union of Brewery Employees. Both parties
had received and studied each other's submissions.

Background to the dispute

The company concerned in the dispute is Riverside Brewing Ltd. It operates
in Birmingham at two sites, Smethwick and Castle Bromwich. In May last
year, the government published guidelines on pay and productivity which
permitted payments to be made during a period of wage restraint, provided
that the money was saved by increased productivity. The company
immediately embarked on a study of all possible methods of improving
productivity and eventually prepared a number of possible methods of
improving productivity and eventually prepared a number of proposals for
the various departments at the two sites.

These proposals were presented to the workforce in October last year. Agreement was sought by the company with the shop stewards representing the workforce in the different sections of the company. These agreements took the form of statements of intent which the shop stewards were asked to sign on behalf of the workers and which they were to implement as soon as possible. The men in the barrel delivery fleet refused to sign any statement of intent and rejected the management's proposals for their section.

The complete set of management proposals became known as the company productivity scheme. It contained a number of anomalies in that not every department had an equal measure of saving, although the scheme provided for total savings to be divided equally among all members. This meant that some departments would in effect be subsidising others. However, despite such anomalies, the scheme was broadly acceptable to all other departments and the changes in working practices were put into effect during the period October to December and payments related to the expected savings were paid to all members of the scheme from 3 October last year.

On 3 November the Distribution Manager, Mr Roberts, sent a letter to the shop stewards of the barrel fleet inviting them to discuss the company productivity proposals again. This invitation resulted in a number of discussions taking place between the shop stewards and Mr Roberts. Eventually a statement of intent was prepared by the shop stewards suggesting a number of changes in working practice which would result in savings to the company. These proposals were considerably different from those made by the management previously and they had to be re-costed. On 19 January this year, the statement of intent was agreed and duly signed. The proposals contained in this statement of intent were considered by the company's central productivity committee and were accepted on 16 February. The committee recommended that the members of the barrel delivery fleet should receive the productivity payments back-dated to 1 January.

On 8 March the shop stewards asked for a meeting with the company to state their case for back-dating of the productivity payments to 1 October last year comparable with the payments received by the rest of the company. This back-dating was refused and shortly afterwards the barrel delivery fleet men began to operate a work to rule and overtime ban. A number of meetings took place and approximately one week later the overtime ban and the work to rule were withdrawn and the matter referred to the disputes procedure. A further meeting was held on 29 March at which the District Official of the Union of Brewing Employees, Mr Jordan, was present. The dispute could not be resolved and it was agreed that the matter should be referred to the Advisory, Conciliation and Arbitration Service. Following further discussions with a member of ACAS it was agreed that the matter would be put to arbitration.

> ## UNION CASE TO THE ARBITRATOR

Union of Brewery Employees

Solidarity House
93 Main Street
Smethwick

Difference between Riverside Brewing Ltd and
Union of Brewery Employees

Barrel delivery fleet:

The dispute involves 85 men, operating the barrel delivery fleet at Smethwick, who claim that they were unfairly excluded from the payment of £4 per week of the company productivity scheme from 3 October to 31 December last year.

They were excluded from payment on the grounds that they refused to sign a notice of intent: the requirements to sign the notice of intent was only applicable to the Smethwick site, and was not conditional at Castle Bromwich.

Therefore:

1. As the scheme was an overall company scheme, the terms of inclusion should have been general.
2. The notice of intent produced by management to the barrel delivery fleet arbitrarily changed the local agreements applicable to working conditions, which was not a feature of any notices of intent or discussions at the other Birmingham site.

    The insistence of management on these arbitrary changes are indicated in Appendix 1 and subsequently re-affirmed in Appendix 2 dated January this year.
3. Within the rules of the scheme as applied at Smethwick, initially the exclusion was on the basis of the whole distribution department. Subsequently, the company accepted inclusion in the scheme of a section within the distribution department, i.e. tanker fleet deliveries, which would indicate discrimination against the barrel deliveries fleet.
4. The final notice of intent signed by the barrel delivery fleet excluded any change to agreements of working conditions, i.e. maximum payload and the introduction of 22 gallon barrels. The application for payment from 3 October and its rejection on the recommendation of the brewery distribution director resulted in an overtime ban being implemented. The dispute was subsequently put back into the Procedure Agreement (Appendix 3).

The Union of Brewery Employees submits that there appears to be discrimination by management at Smethwick against 85 members of the barrel delivery fleet by their exclusion from the company productivity deal and payment of £4.00 per week from 3 October last year, by a refusal to discuss proposals with this section of membership in the same way as was conducted with every other sector covered by the deal within the Birmingham area.

On 31 December, over 2000 employees (including 100 part-timers) were receiving the bonus, the only exclusion being our membership involved in this dispute.

Signed

C. Jordan
Group Secretary

COMPANY CASE TO THE ARBITRATOR

Riverside Brewing Ltd
Smethwick Brewery
Dispute concerning productivity payments
Barrel delivery fleet

Background to dispute: summary statement

1.1   This dispute is concerned with a claim by the Smethwick barrel delivery fleet for the back-dating to 1 October last year of the Riverside brewing productivity payment (£4 per man per week) despite the fact that an agreed statement of intent relating to changes in working practices was not signed until 19 January this year.

1.2   At the opening of productivity discussions at the beginning of October last all staff and employees in Riverside Brewing Ltd, including Smethwick retail fleet (barrel and tankers), were approached through their representatives by individual management teams. The objective was to define changes in working practices which would result in financial gains capable of being translated into self-financing productivity payments.

1.3   The agreed changes in working practices were documented in departmental statements of intent, the cost gains for each calculated, and then the total cost gain for Birmingham defined. This total 'pot' was the amount to be used for productivity payments. This did mean that some departments were contributing more than others and therefore that not all departments were totally self-financed.

1.4 It should be noted that in parallel with the overall Riverside brewing productivity scheme, the Smethwick barrel delivery fleet were pursuing, and achieved, a separate productivity deal associated with difficult call payments. An agreement on this was reached on 21 October last year.

1.5 A proposed statement of intent for inclusion with the Riverside Brewing productivity scheme, based on carrying additional barrels on a vehicle was submitted by the distribution department management to the delivery fleets shop stewards. This was rejected, and no positive alternative proposals were forthcoming from the shop stewards.

1.6 In order to give every opportunity to the Smethwick delivery fleets to join the company scheme, the Smethwick distribution manager wrote to the shop stewards on 3 November, inviting more discussion.

1.7 The meeting of the Productivity Central Committee, who were to discuss the statements of intent, was delayed to allow for the late inclusion of the Smethwick delivery fleet.

1.8 A positive response came from the tanker fleet shop stewards, and subsequently a statement of intent for this section was formulated in time for inclusion in the first quarter of the productivity scheme.

1.9 No response came from the barrel shop stewards.

1.10 Therefore the position at this stage was that approximately 2000 people on two major sites were covered by the company productivity scheme from 1 October, and 85 (i.e. Smethwick barrel fleet) were outside this scheme, but were paid separate productivity payments from 13 October.

1.11 In mid-December, the barrel shop stewards decided to approach management with a more positive attitude, and discussions then took place, from which resulted a proposed statement of intent. This statement of intent was subsequently ratified by the barrel fleet and signed and submitted on 19 January this year.

1.12 The company's Productivity Committee accepted the proposals made, and back-dated the productivity payments to the start of the second quarter, i.e. 1 January this year.

Barrel fleet statement of intent

1.0 Barrel fleet statement of intent

The statement of intent from the barrel fleet and the costing and description of each item are shown on the following pages.

2.1   Comments

2.2   The final statement of intent was not discussed and signed until the period mid-December last year to mid-January this year.

2.3   Of the eleven items submitted, six produced a financial gain which could be transferred to productivity payments.

2.4   Of the six contributing items, only two are changes in working practices (Items 2 and 4).

2.5   The other four items, one of which is the single most significant financial contributor, were continuing practices, all of which started prior to 1 August, but practices outside normal working patterns and on short term agreements.

The statement of intent transferred these working practices from short term agreements to a permanent basis, and were thus accepted from that time for productivity payment purposes.

ASSOCIATED DOCUMENTS

Riverside Brewing Ltd Productivity Scheme

5 September

1. The scheme

1.1 The scheme is designed to be in accord with the guidelines agreed by the government and the TUC.

1.2 There will be a fund realised by savings obtained by productivity improvements and/or cost reductions agreed and resulting from employee/company co-operation.

1.3 The savings contributed to the fund will be monitored quarterly in line with the company's accounting practice.

1.4 The eligibility of savings arising from proposals not currently listed as already agreed to become part of the fund will be assessed by the financial director.

1.5 The scheme will operate from 3 October to at least 1 May. Prior to the later date the scheme will be reviewed by the Central Productivity Committee.

1.6 Any member of the Central Productivity Committee may request a meeting of the committee during the period of operation of the scheme.

2. Eligibility

2.1 75 per cent of the fund will be distributed in equal portions to all permanent employees of Riverside Brewing except the managing director subject only to the following:

(a) part-time employees will receive a sum pro rata to their normal working hours;

(b) personnel who are absent for one day or more without authorisation will not qualify for any productivity payment for the week in which the absence occurs. Unauthorised absence is defined as absence for which:

● a doctor's certificate is not produced to the company or
● the manager's approval has not been obtained.

(c) Employees leaving the company's employment will have no claim on the fund after the date of termination of employment.

2.2 The remaining 25 per cent of the fund will be retained by the company as a contribution to maintain present price levels and reduce inflation.

3. Payments

3.1 Payments will be made weekly or monthly, as appropriate, and initially at the rate of £4.00 per week, effective 3 October.

3.2 Savings will be monitored following the end of the above period and the level of payment thereafter reviewed.

4. Information on savings realised

Information as necessary to enable the scheme to be reviewed by the Central Productivity Committee will be distributed to members of that committee.

Signed

B. C. Marlow
Brewing and Distribution Director

Initial Statement of Proposals

Self-financing productivity bargaining

Proposal:

That if the remuneration is acceptable, the two delivery fleets will:

Barrels

1. Take out an additional seven pieces per 5.9 ton load.
2. Agree to a planning horizon of 495 work units.

Tankers

1. Carry a CO_2 blanket.
2. Accept in the future non-standard vehicles.

The return to the deliveries fleets will be:

1. A productivity payment per man per week – the level of payment to be defined.
2. The limitation of establishment to maintain earnings potential.

A. L. Roberts
Distribution Manager

10 October

Distribution Department
Productivity bargaining

Smethwick retail deliveries fleets – statement of intent

It is the intention of the Smethwick retail deliveries fleets *not* to participate in the Riverside Brewing's self-financing productivity bargain.

This intention was registered after a meeting on 11 October, of all the employees involved.

The items put to the retail deliveries fleet are attached.

A. L. Roberts
Distribution Manager

Diary of main events during productivity discussions

Early October	Discussions with shop stewards regarding productivity. Proposal relating to additional barrels per load evaluated with stewards.
11 October	Shop stewards meeting with barrel and tanker fleets, discussed statement of intent for company productivity.
	At this time the proposals were to cover both barrel and tanker fleets and had been evaluated to give a return of about £5.00 per week.
	Meeting rejected this proposal.
3 November	Letter sent by A. L. Roberts to shop stewards inviting them to re-discuss productivity questions.
1 December	From response by tanker stewards, discussions held with tanker men and statement of intent formulated.
22 December	Draft statement of intent submitted by barrel delivery stewards.
11 January	Roberts discussed productivity and statement of intent with barrel fleet.
19 January	Statement of intent signed and submitted.
16 February	Central Productivity Committee accept statement of intent from barrel delivery fleet.

Riverside Brewing Ltd

15 March

Dear

Work to Rule

I am very concerned regarding the breakdown in communication that appears to be causing our current problems.

Obviously you must feel equally concerned, as the loss of overtime, additional loads and the planned Saturday and Sunday overtime this weekend will cost more than your claim for back-payment, which totals £52.

For this reason I am taking the unusual step of writing to you.

What may not be understood is that the company **is not in a position to agree back-payment**. All productivity schemes are open to examination by the incomes division of the Department of Employment, who ensure that they conform to government guidelines.

The brewing industry is currently under public scrutiny. Two companies have already been approached by the incomes division, and we have been informed that our scheme will also be examined.

Auditors would have to consider your reluctance to join the original scheme in November, despite my written request to your stewards to re-discuss the original statement of intent and your subsequent self-finance scheme for difficult jobs. As a result, you did not decide to enter the scheme until January this year and your statement of intent was eventually signed on 19 January.

At the moment, I see no way out of the problem, as it is **inconceivable** that back-dating will be allowed, and in the meantime your earnings and company trade are suffering. Therefore, the sooner we can sort this out within company/trade union procedures, the better.

I am writing with the knowledge of your stewards, as this is the fastest way I can communicate with all of you, in the hope that you may re-consider your position before the weekend.

Yours sincerely

A. L. Roberts
Distribution Manager

20th March

We, the Smethwick barrel fleet are in a 'failure to agree' situation with the management in that we have been paid the £4 per week company productivity payment from 1 January.

The dispute is caused by the fact that we believe we are entitled to payment from 1 October when the scheme started.

W. Bainbridge
N. Thomson
M. R. Smyth

Shop Stewards
UBE

A. L. Roberts
Distribution Manager

Riverside Brewing Ltd

Memorandum

From A. L. Roberts

To: Mr H. Brown
Mr R. Timpson
Mr T. Neil

Date: 3 November

cc: Mr B. C. Marlow

Birmingham self-financing productivity bargain

You will remember that over the past three or four weeks, we have been talking in some detail about this Birmingham self-financing productivity scheme, and the participation of the Smethwick retail fleets.

While knowing that the proposals were rejected by the fleet members, can I say that the door is not closed, and that the option to join in is still open, should the members wish to re-consider, within the next seven days.

I attach a further copy of the proposals we made, and I am prepared to re-discuss these with you.

A. L. Roberts
Distribution Manager

AHTH/dva

Smethwick Brewery

Statement of intent – productivity bargaining

Smethwick barrel

The retail delivery fleet agrees to:

1. Unload empties at various points in the yard as opposed to the original three points, i.e. Guinness, CO_2, Beer, Cider and Ullage.
2. Back-stack empties three high in the appropriate areas.
3. Drive vehicles not designed for barrel delivery.
4. Continue four start times to enable more three turn days to be planned.
5. Handle excess amounts of five gallon barrels at peak periods.
6. To reject leakers at the loading bank to prevent these being returned.
7. Operate vehicles without CO_2 racks – saving capital expenditure.
8. Exercise more care in delivering to save damage at premises, to containers and to goods.
9. Vet each load to determine the most efficient route to save fuel.
10. Launder own clothing to save revenue expenditure.

Finalised costing of barrel statement of intent and definition of supporting items

Item no.		Annual gains
1.	Established practice. No financial gain.	£0000
2.	Warehouse gain. Start 20 January.	£1500
3.	Existing practice from mid-summer, but replacement vehicles taken off last year's budget on 19 January this year.	
	Value at two vehicles × £8,000 × 10%.	£1600
4.	No financial gain.	£0000
5.	Practice started May last year to cover summer peak periods. Continued on short term agreement until after Christmas. New agreement for productivity statement of intent reached 19 January this year.	£1400
6.	Statement of existing responsibility.	£0000
7.	No vehicles are fitted with CO_2 racks. Planned for this year. Budget cancelled 19 January. One-off gain: 40 vehicles × £200 × 10%.	£800
8.	Statement of existing responsibility.	£0000

9. Statement of existing responsibility.   £0000
10. Laundering of protective clothing has been carried
    out by crew members for a number of years, although
    finance in budget to cover this. Budget item cancelled
    19 January – gain.   £1600

                                                    Total   £19 900

Steps in dispute action this year

                                                          31 March

8 March   Meeting: shop steward/brewing and distribution director/senior
steward/distribution manager. Stewards stated case for back-
dating; brewing and distribution director stated he could not
recommend payment from 1 October.

13 March   Stewards met men to relay information – as a result:

            Action out of procedure:
            - work to rule
            - overtime ban
            - fleet 'blacked' anyone who had been paid from 1 October i.e. tanker men and recruits

15 March   Meeting: distribution manager/stewards to review situation and
to attempt to get dispute into procedure.

16 March   Letter sent to men.

17 March   6.15 a.m.   Meeting: distribution manager/personnel manager/
shop stewards. Distribution manager attempted to
'keep door open' for weekend working and try
again to get into procedure.

            7.00 a.m.   Meeting: shop stewards/men – no reaction,
continue to work to rule – no return procedure.

            11.30 a.m. Meeting: deputy managing director/brewing
and distribution director/personnel manager/
distribution manager/senior shop stewards.

            Recommendation to return to status quo and to
re-convene as early as possible. A Smethwick
Productivity Committee to review barrel deliveries
case.

            2.35 p.m.   Meeting: shop stewards/men – return to
procedure (overtime ban still on).

(*Note:*   2.40 p.m. distribution manager had to cancel weekend overtime
option because of lack of time to organise.)

20 March Meeting: shop stewards/men – continue overtime ban.
21 March Distribution manager/men – explained position of productivity.

Meeting took place   7.05 to 8.15 a.m.
Stewards continued   8.15 to 8.40 a.m.

After holding a two hour meeting (with prior management consent) the men refused to do six hours work to complete the day, demanding only four hours work. When six hours was issued they walked off the job, returning the next day.

Failure to agree handed to deliveries manager at 8.50 a.m.

Meeting: brewing and distribution director/senior brewery union stewards/senior craft steward. Decision to put this dispute through normal grievance and conciliation procedure. District official called in for 29 March.

22 March Meeting: shop stewards/distribution manager. Stewards agreed to recommend to men to return to status quo, including normal overtime working – accepted by men.
23 March No additional loads due to Saturday working agreement.
29 March Meeting: brewing and distribution director/distribution manager/personnel manager/district official/senior shop steward/shop stewards – dispute not resolved referred to ACAS.

Signed
A. L. Roberts
Distribution Manager

Riverside Brewing Ltd

Memorandum

From: A. L. Roberts

Date: 10 January

To: Mr T. Neil
Mr H. Brown
Mr R. Timpson
cc: Mr S. Berry
Mr B. C. Marlow

SELF-FINANCING PRODUCTIVITY AGREEMENT

These notes summarise the discussions which we have had over the past four weeks on this subject:

1. The cost of paying the members of the barrel fleet at the current

company productivity bargain rate of £4 per man per week would be approximately £17 000 per annum.

2. In order for this payment to be 'self-financing' it is necessary to either generate additional, or change existing, activities so that this amount of money is created for payment.

3. The 'self-financing' rule is not a company rule, but one from the Incomes Division of the Department of Employment, who are monitoring our scheme.

4. I have already defined for you that in terms of additional payload. It will be necessary to carry four additional barrels per load to self-finance £4 per week for the members of the barrel deliveries fleet.

5. Similarly, the acceptance of handling 22 gallon barrels would positively contribute to the ability of the Company to meet trade demands, and therefore would be seen as self-financing.

6. The draft statement of intent submitted by you contains a number of items which, in fact, are not changes but are continuations of existing practices, and regrettably the Incomes Division specifically exclude continuing practices.

7. Once a statement of intent has been approved by the members of the barrel fleet, it will be submitted to the Central Productivity Committee. This body is comprised of both management and trade union representatives, and it is this committee which will decide whether or not the statement of intent makes the barrel delivery fleet eligible for entry into the company's scheme.

A. L. Roberts
Distribution Manager

Questions

1 Do you think the productivity scheme is an appropriate one?
2 Were the barrel fleet members justified in opting out of the scheme when most of the workforce accepted it?
3 Should the barrel fleet receive the £4 payments from 3 October or 1 January?

Arbitration between BAIRD LTD

and

the TECHNICIANS AND SUPERVISORS UNION

(concerning the job grading of technical officers and supervisors)

Terms of reference

The terms of reference agreed by both parties were:

Job grading: to define the relationship with other jobs in the company's monthly paid staff's joint agreed job evaluation grade structure in respect of:

1. Manufacturing instructions officer
2. Materials testing officer
3. Quality control supervisor

Documentation

The arbitrator received a full statement of the case from Baird Ltd. This was supported by copies of relevant letters and extracts from the job descriptions agreed by the joint management and union grading panel. He also received a submission from the Technicians and Supervisors Union together with a detailed set of job descriptions and copies of the relevant organisation charts.

Both parties had received and studied each other's submissions.

Background to the dispute

Baird Ltd manufactures brake pads, brake linings and friction materials. The company has had a factory in Glasgow for nearly 80 years and a factory in Motherwell for about 12 years.

The company set up a joint management and union panel which reported in April 1978. This joint panel recommended that the manufacturing instructions officer should be Grade 5, that the materials testing officer should be Grade 6, and that four jobs at Motherwell and one at Glasgow concerned with supervision and quality control be assessed as Grade 7 or 8. This was the first time a job grading scheme has been introduced at management and supervisory level within the Baird company.

The job gradings which are the subject of the current dispute were all appealed shortly after the joint management union panel reported. This appeal resulted in the following changes of grade.

In July 1978, the Grade of manufacturing instructions officer was raised from 5 to 6 and that of the materials testing officer from 6 to 7. With respect to the four inspection quality control jobs at Motherwell and the similar job at Glasgow, a complete review of these jobs was effected and by July 1979 the four jobs at Motherwell were combined as supervisor, quality control, and awarded Grade 9. The similar job at Glasgow was also described as supervisor, quality control, and similarly awarded Grade 9.

At Glasgow the quality control supervisors had been responsible for a large number of quality examiners. Management briefly introduced a change which allocated the examiners to production sections, relieving the supervisors of much of their previous responsibility. In September 1979, responsibility for examiners was re-assumed by the supervisors and, following negotiations, a single payment of £500 was made to supervisors for re-establishing these controls.

During 1978 and 1979 a large number of appeals to the proposed gradings was considered. Most of these were satisfactorily resolved with the exception of those mentioned above. In the case of the three jobs under consideration by the arbitrator the following changes took place. Upon consideration of the appeal on behalf of the manufacturing instructions officer the management proposed an upgrading from 6 to 7. The Technicians and Supervisors Union argues that the responsibilities of this particular job are commensurate with others in the plant accorded Grade 8 and have not accepted Grade 7 for this job. A careful examination of the duties and responsibilities of the materials testing officer indicated that the job was, in the management's opinion, correctly assessed at Grade 7, but that some aspects of the work were closer to the duties of Grade 8. The management accordingly proposed that this job should be upgraded from 7 to 8 but the union have refused and have requested a change to Grade 9.

The situation with respect to the quality control supervisors is more complicated since the supervisors at Motherwell feel that the £500 extra payment made to their colleagues at Glasgow represents an indication that the responsibilities of the job are higher than Grade 9. The company on its part argues that this one-time payment was concerned with re-establishing control over examiners rather than payment for the ongoing duties of these supervisors. Both Motherwell and Glasgow quality control supervisors argue that their responsibilities are commensurate with section managers who are placed on Grade 10 and accordingly they ask for upgrading from 9 to 10.

UNION CASE TO THE ARBITRATOR

Submission to ACAS arbitrator for manufacturing Instructions officer, materials testing officer and quality control supervisor

Introduction

The three cases in the job grading dispute are all in the research division of Baird Ltd.

They are part of a job grading complaint for the whole of the division (over 100 people) present since job grading was introduced in April 1978. After a working party in late 1979, the company agreed with the complaints and in 1980, a specialist structure was brought in to cover Grades 9 and 10. This left approximately 12 people in grades below 9 who were still in dispute. Since then, some re-grading/retirement/leaving has taken place and the present disputed jobs involve six people on Grades 6 and 7.

Manufacturing instructions officer

The following documents were submitted:

Reference

1. Job description, no. 6032 dated June 1978.
2. Job description ungraded dated August 1980.
3. Job description, no. 9102 dated February 1979 – senior manufacturing instructions officer.

References 1 and 2 both describe the job, with Reference 2 being the updated version. The crux of the job is described in Reference 2, parts (a) and (b) of section 3. However, the vast scope and technical nature are brought out more in Reference 1.

The job is divided into three areas (three people) and the total training period for the three areas is many years. The job holders must be able to communicate with and understand highly specialist individuals, such as physicists, chemists and engineers. They are not expected to understand the theories or chemistry of the processes but must have a suitable background to understand the reasonings, hence the desirability of HNC in appropriate subjects. The third job is a new job, presently unfilled, for a person to work at our Motherwell factory, doing similar functions to those at Glasgow. This job has been graded freely by the company and has been graded at 9. The main difference is that, although he/she is expected to observe production and point out any deviations, he/she is not allowed to actually put them right him/herself. This feature is also a part of the Grade 6 job.

Materials testing officer

The following documents were submitted:

Reference

4. Job description assistant material technologist, no. 7070, dated early 1978.
5. Job description materials testing officer, ungraded, dated August 1980.
6. Job description technical officer in quality control, no. 9076, dated April 1978.

Reference 4 is the original job description which does not describe the job and is not correct since material technologists are involved in developing new materials and assistant material technologists work alongside them, not doing physical tests in a physics laboratory. Reference 5 is the latest agreed job description, which accurately describes the job. Reference 6 is a Grade 9 job in our QC department, which is of a similar nature in that it involves doing tests on raw materials and products, sometimes developing new tests. The new tests needed in the materials testing job are quite often of a novel nature since the problems arise in the development of new materials.

Quality control supervisors

This case will be presented at the arbitration hearing.

| COMPANY CASE TO THE ARBITRATOR |

Arbitration of job grading differences

between Baird Limited and

The Technicians and Supervisors Union

1. **Manufacturing instructions officer**

2. **Materials testing officer**

Additional case:

3. **(a) Supervisor quality control, Motherwell**

   (b) Supervisor quality control, Glasgow

History and background to the dispute

1. Manufacturing instructions officer

1.1 Two jobs were originally evaluated by a joint management/union panel in April 1978, both resulting in Grade 5.

Job no. 5046: technical writer – manufacturing instructions;

Job no. 5043: technical officer – calculations and clerical.

1.2 Following an appeal by the job holders, a new job description was submitted combining the two jobs. This was upgraded to Grade 6 in July 1978: job no. 6032: technical data processing officer.

1.3 A new appeal was made in February 1979, again supported by some changes in work content. In reviewing the appeal, a new job description was submitted in August 1976, further considerations were given to comparisons with other jobs and it was proposed to upgrade the job again to Grade 7. This proposal has not yet been accepted; claims have been made for Grade 8.

1.4 In accordance with the agreed procedure this matter was referred to the senior personnel manager. The case was discussed at a meeting with the district officer of TSU and the company on 13 September 1979.

Following this meeting further investigations were made and the senior personnel manager considered that in view of all the relevant information available, the correct grading for this job should be Grade 7.

2. Materials testing officer

2.1 The job was originally evaluated Grade 6 by the joint management/ union panel in April 1978: job no. 6010: materials testing officer (three job descriptions).

2.2 Following many appeals against job grading in the technical division, a new job structure was introduced in the division, reducing the number of jobs from 40 to 15. This took place in July 1978, and resulted in the above job being re-titled 'assistant material technologist'; job no. 7070 (Grade 7).

2.3 A further appeal was made in June 1979, supported by a revised job description. The revised job description did not indicate a change in job content compared with the original job descriptions made in April 1978. In dealing with the appeal, comparisons were made with other jobs which had been up-graded as a result of appeals. These comparisons showed that the true position of the job was somewhere between Grade 7 and Grade 8.

2.4 In accordance with the agreed procedure this matter was referred to the senior personnel manager. The case was discussed at a meeting with the district officer of TSU and the company on 13 September 1979.

Following this meeting, further investigations were made and the senior personnel manager considered that in case of doubt we should err on the generous side, and subsequently Grade 8 was offered. So far however, this offer has not yet been accepted.

3. Supervisor quality control, Motherwell and supervisor quality control, Glasgow

3.1 Four job descriptions were originally evaluated by a joint management/ union panel in April 1978:
Supervisor standards inspection, Motherwell (Grade 7);
Supervisor quality control, Motherwell (Grade 8);
Supervisor final inspection, Motherwell (Grade 8);
Quality surveyor, Glasgow (Grade 8).

3.2 Appeals supported by new job descriptions resulted in upgrading to Grade 9 with effect from July 1979. The four jobs at Motherwell were combined into one job:
(a)   Supervisor quality control, Motherwell;
(b)   Supervisor quality control, Glasgow.

3.3 At the Glasgow factory the supervisors quality control were responsible for 100 examiners; 80 of the examiners were allocated to production sections. The management of the production sections were responsible for administration only.

In some areas of the factory the administration was passed back to supervisors quality control; additional payments were made for taking on these duties from September 1979.

3.4   A new job description was submitted in February 1980, this transferred the total responsibilities for the 80 examiners to supervisors quality control.

After many meetings agreement was reached between Mr McDermott (Personnel Manager) and Mr Kelly (Divisional Officer) on 25 April 1980, that the correct grade for this job is Grade 9.

3.5   At the Motherwell factory the Supervisors Quality Control have had full management of 65 examiners all the time.

3.6   A joint agreed note was signed on behalf of the management and on behalf of TSU on 20 June 1980.

The company and its products

Union representation

1.1   Baird Ltd manufactures brake pads, brake linings and friction materials. It has factories at Glasgow and Motherwell.

1.2   Union representation:

Hourly paid factory employees   T&GWU
Hourly paid tradesmen   CSEU
Weekly paid staff (Grades 1–5)   ACTSS

Monthly paid senior staff (Grades 6–10) are represented in the main by TSU while a small number of engineers are represented by TASS; some works laboratory staff and the vehicles testing officers are represented by ACTSS.

Arguments opposing the claims

Job evaluation calls for a reasoned assessment of fact to fairly determine the relative positions of jobs in relation to other jobs. This calls for evaluators from management and the union to adopt a style that will achieve the objectives in an acceptable manner without pressure. Unfortunately the outside pressure from the union side is causing concern for the credibility of the scheme.

1.   Manufacturing instructions officer

1.1   Although this job has been described in a number of job descriptions, the job title has changed. It is recognised that the joint panel in 1978 may have assessed this job on the low side, which has been shown by moving the job from Grade 5 to Grade 6.

In no way can it be seen that this job is in excess of Grade 7 when compared with other jobs.

Submitted for comparison purposes were the following job descriptions:

Job no. 7051: computer programmer stage II (Grade 7);
Job no. 7106: insurance and secretarial officer (Grade 7).

2.   Materials testing officer

2.1   In this case the new job description does not indicate a change in the job from the descriptions submitted to the original joint evaluation panel.

While comparing this job with other jobs that have been upgraded as a result of appeals, the management considers that the job was at the higher end of Grade 7. However, as some doubt existed, Grade 8 was offered. In no way can justification be found for this job to be given a higher grade.

Submitted for comparison purposes were the following job descriptions:

Job no. 8101: systems analyst stage II (Grade 8);
Job no. 8106: technical officer workshops (Grade 8).

3.   Supervisor quality control

Agreement was reached on 25 April 1980 that the correct grade for this job is Grade 9.

Paragraph 2.3 of the joint agreed note clearly states:

'It is agreed that the job of quality control supervisor remains at Grade 9. This means that the supervisors' claim for upgrading is now dropped and the union will not back any future claim for upgrading this job on the basis of the attached job description.'

Summary of the case

1.   The management submissions ask the arbitrator to consider:
1.2   In the case of the 'manufacturing instructions officer' that Grade 7 offered is the correct assessment of the job in relation to other jobs.
1.3   In respect of the 'materials testing officer' that Grade 8 offered is the correct assessment of the job in relation to other jobs.
1.4   In the case of the 'supervisor quality control' that Grade 9 is the correct assessment of the job.

ASSOCIATED DOCUMENTS

Appendix 1

Agreement between

the Technicians and Supervisors Union

and Baird Ltd

1. Agreement was reached on 15 April 1978, between Baird Ltd and the staff unions on the job evaluation exercise carried out between the management and the unions.
2. At the final meeting with the unions, it was agreed that in the event of a senior staff member being dissatisfied with his job grade, he would be allowed to submit an appeal to his immediate superior explaining why he considered the grading of his job to be incorrect. The manager will, in turn, inform the personnel department.
3. In order to replace the former job grading panel on the assessment of new jobs or on the basis of re-grading, a meeting would take place between the job evaluation officer on behalf of the company and the appointed monthly-paid staff representative to compare the new job descriptions with those of similar jobs elsewhere in the company. The job description will, of course, have had its origin in that particular section through the departmental head and have been agreed by the job holder.

The decision of the newly constituted procedure will, of course, be communicated back to the job holder through the head of department.

If there is still no agreement at this stage, then the matter shall be dealt with in the procedure.

Signed on behalf of the management

Date

Signed on behalf of the union

Date

Job Description:

Manufacturing Instructions Officer

[*Before this job description is completed, reference should be made to the separate notes for guidance.*]

1. Job title: Manufacturing Instructions (MI) Officer

Department: Technical Administration.
Responsible to: Manager of Manufacturing Instructions Section.

Note: an organisation chart showing the relationship of the job to other positions should also be attached (*see* Appendix 1).

2. Purpose:

To convert technical information to formal manufacturing instructions (MI) for use by various departments at Glasgow and Motherwell for the manufacture of products against customers' orders and for preparing quotations for new business. Baird MI is also the basis for overseas manufacture by both Baird companies and licensees.

3. Main functions (accountabilities):

(a)   receive, acquire and continuously update all the information needed for the following groups of MI and publish this information in a form appropriate to the needs of user departments:

- mix instructions
- product instructions
- process instructions
- raw material specifications
- standard control methods

(b)   compile graphs, formulae and prepared tables in support of MI;
(c)   publish edited extracts of MI (particularly mix instructions) for use by production operatives;
(d)   prepare and publish change notes including a historical record of the background to the change;
(e)   monitor the temporary alteration note scheme to ensure that all temporary MI changes are either confirmed or cancelled on expiry;
(f)   prepare and publish proposed manufacturing procedures (PMP) incorporating technical division and facilities information for use by costing and planning departments in providing factory costs and delivery promises against QPs and sales promotion projects;

(g)   maintain the standard and special product register and provide an information service to sales on the availability of MI for new sizes outside the standard product register;
(h)   maintain internal information lists for use by technical staff;
(i)   provide input data for the computer mix programme;
(j)   publish methods procedures and plant instructions for facilities after scrutinising for conflict with MI.

4. Scope and dimensions

No. of Employees

(a)   supervision and management control
      degree of control
      management supervisor or specialist
      technical skilled manual or clerical
      routine manual or clerical
      reporting directly
      through subordinates
      indirectly controlled
(b)   financial and other dimensions: as MI is the basis for the company's manufacturing operations, errors and omissions can lead to serious losses affecting material, plant, equipment, labour, health/safety and customer goodwill. Confidentiality and security of MI are vital;
(c)   scope and restraint: the MI officer will need to give instructions to the distributions clerk and to the technical typists and will assist with training of new staff, both within the department, and as part of the induction programme for management and accountancy trainees. There are standards of presentation for MI and all drafts are checked for accuracy and security before issue. However, the job holder is expected to pioneer improvements in the content and format of MI and to query all anomalies and deficiencies, consulting the technical departments as appropriate.

5. Relationships:

(a)   within the company, relationships involve the technical division, facilities, production and quality control at Glasgow and Motherwell together with sales, costing and purchase. Approximately half the contacts are above Grade 10 and the remainder mainly in the range 8–10;
(b)   outside the company relationships are infrequent but could include visits to other companies to exchange ideas on MI systems, etc.

6. Skills, experience and qualifications (to be completed by manager of the position):

(a) essential: a minimum of GCE 'O' level English language and maths or the equivalent plus four years' experience in a technical or production position in Baird;

(b) desirable: HNC in appropriate subjects.

7. Other information:

(a) the job holder must be capable of adopting a sound analytical approach to the job and by means of creative thinking, be able to recognise how improvements in one group of instructions can be extended to other groups;

(b) an experienced MI officer has a unique knowledge of the total information requirements of MI users and is thus able to advise technical staff on the amount of detail needed.

8. Concurrences

Description prepared by: *Description approved by*:

_____   _____
(Analyst/Job Holder)   (Line Supervisor)
date   date

Agreed by:

_____   _____
(Job Holder/Analyst)   (Functional Head, if appropriate)
date   date

Appendix 1

Organisation Chart –
Technical Administration Department

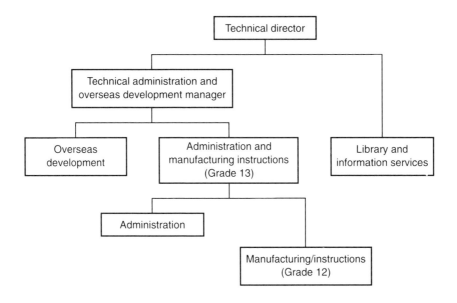

Job Description:

Materials Testing Officer

[Before this job description is completed, reference should be made to the separate notes for guidance.]

1. Job title: Materials Testing Officer

Department: Materials Testing.
Responsible to: DM Materials Testing

Note: an organisation chart showing the relationship of the job to other positions should also be attached (*see* Appendix 2).

2. Purpose:

To investigate all manner of problems associated with physical properties of raw materials, semi-finished and finished products, including brake and clutch components:

(a) devise standard and specialised test procedures where none exist;
(b) carry out testing and calculate and record the results;
(c) advise formulators and technical sales of results and their significance;
(d) determine standard test procedures for quality control purposes.

3. Main functions (accountabilities):

(a) devise and carry out tests for products and establish acceptable standards for manufacture;
(b) devise and carry out tests of Ferodo and competitors' products for technical sales and formulators;
(c) carry out tests on complete brake and clutch assemblies to determine applied loads in vehicle or machine tests;
(d) adapt existing test apparatus and supplement with new devices in order to carry out tests;
(e) measure properties of engineering components for engineering design staff in the development of plant;
(f) process test results, analyse and compile reports.

4. Scope and dimensions

No. of employees

(a) supervision and management control
degree of control
management supervisor or specialist

technical skilled manual or clerical
routine manual or clerical
reporting directly
through subordinates
indirectly controlled

(b)   financial and other dimensions: the job holder continually uses expensive and sometimes delicate equipment (up to £10 000). Damage due to negligence means costly repairs and the loss of that particular facility for the time taken to carry out repairs.

Results which for any reason are erroneous can lead to:

- loss of test machine time, e.g. approximately £200 per test;
- loss of vehicle test time, e.g. approximately £800 per test;
- loss of business presently held;
- loss of future business;
- accidents.

Thus the job holder must ensure that all work carried out is accurate and any equipment used is correctly calibrated. There is also the freedom to recommend the acquisition of new equipment.

(c)   scope and restraint: every experimental material devised in technical division is subjected to physical property tests such as density, hardness, tensile, compressive, bending, shear strength and thermal stability. Only the most promising materials progress to the dynamometer and vehicle testing. Certain tests require high load and temperatures, hence safety procedures must be strictly followed.

In the absence of standard methods of testing, new techniques are devised. Frequently the customer's method of testing has to be challenged.

Innovation and creative ability are requirements of the job. Work must conform to safety, professional and ethical standards. Calculations of results in appropriate units require the use of a desk top calculator or Hewlett-Packard programmable minicomputer.

The issue of reports and results to respective authors gives advice and opinions on the tests and data obtained.

The job also involves maintaining a comprehensive file of information on materials tested, used by publicity, for data sheets and to determine trends in standards.

The work is controlled by divisional and technical sales priorities.

Technical problems such as chemical analysis are referred to others.

The job holder is expected to work without supervision though more expert technical assistance is available.

5. Relationships:

(a)   within the company, relationships involve the technical sales staff, technical division staff, factory staff and operatives;

(b)   outside the company, relationships involve customers.

6. Skills, experience and qualifications (to be completed by manager of the position): practical light engineering skills and experience with a basic knowledge of maths and mechanics. They must be alert and have an enquiring mind

(a)   essential: experience in manufacturing and testing of Baird materials;

(b)   desirable: should have a basic knowledge of chemistry and physics.

7. Other information

8. Concurrences

Description prepared by: *Description approved by*:

_____   _____

(Analyst/Job Holder)   (Line Supervisor)
date   date

Agreed by:

_____   _____

(Job Holder/Analyst)   (Functional Head, if appropriate)
date   date

Appendix 2

Organisation Chart –

Materials Testing Department

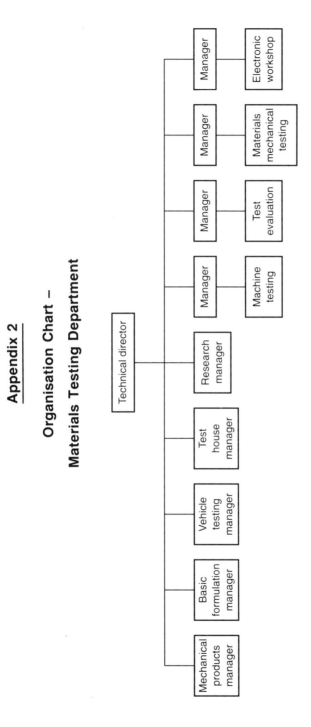

Job Description:

Supervisor (Glasgow)

[*Before this job description is completed, reference should be made to the separate notes for guidance.*]

1. Job title: Supervisor

Department: Quality Control
Responsible to: Chief Inspector, Glasgow

Note: an organisation chart showing the relationship of the job to other positions should also be attached (*see* Appendix 3).

2. Purpose:

(a) to organise, administer and control an inspection force covering the whole factory on a 24 hour basis;
(b) to provide an effective technical supervision of inspection and control functions and of all matters affecting physical quality of products and of other items sold by the company; to carry out short term investigations on fault situations and to ensure that effective remedial action is generated; to act as inspector in charge on night shift or at other times when the Chief Inspector is not present.

3. Main functions (accountabilities)

(a) *quality*: the key concern is the maintenance of the required condition and quality level of products and parts but with maximum cost effectiveness; to have access to products and parts at all stages for this purpose so as to take action at the earliest possible stage;
(b) *output*: he/she is concerned with the entire output of the company: to ensure that a sufficient and competent inspection force is available and to administer it effectively; to exercise control over inspection labour in order to meet the demand for both priority and quantity targets as indicated by production management; to organise redeployment of examiners as necessary, according to fluctuations of production flow and absenteeism, etc.;
(c) *inspection instructions*: to develop detailed procedures for inspection tasks, suitable for valid estimation of reliability, while providing adequate detail for the establishment of work values;
(d) *training*: in conjunction with the training department, to arrange and participate in the training of examiners in such a manner that the quality department can have full confidence in its competence;

(e) *control*: principal controls are the departmental budgets and the quality levels achieved, as displayed in the extent of rejections and of customer reports and complaints. Periodic appraisal statements by customers are becoming a common feature, surveying the general quality performance;

(f) *human relations*: conventional industrial relations have a significant impact and general good human relations have to be maintained in this area of activity where any technical failure creates problems for the customers. Maintenance of the goodwill of examiners is essential to technical success.

The supervisor is required to promote the highest possible standard of industrial relations and ensure that all relevant regulations and agreements are observed;

(g) to administer and operate the whole inspection force, making changes in sectional allocations as necessary to meet the needs of production quantities, training programmes or absence of key examiners, etc.; to deal with immediate problems in the area of operation throughout the whole shift;

(h) *development – new types of products*: to assist development staff in establishing new products and procedures by judgments and recommendations on any unacceptable reject pattern; to ensure that an adequate specification is established and to co-ordinate the setting up of visual standards;

(i) *management cover*: to ensure adequate quality management cover for the factory is maintained at all times. This involves among other things, operating as direct deputy for the chief inspector outside normal day hours;

(j) *payment systems*: in connection with new payment systems in production, linked with 'good' products, responsibility is squarely on the inspection supervisor to ensure that defects are correctly described and that examiners do not respond to pressure to classify rejects in any biased manner in connection with the operators' incentive scheme.

4. Scope and dimensions

(a) *supervision and management*: full administrative and technical responsibility for the whole inspection force of 90–100 examiners, operating throughout the factory and on a 24 hour basis;

(b) *financial and other dimensions*:

- the supervisors carry the immediate and day to day responsibility for physical and dimensional quality of the whole production of the Glasgow factories valued at factory cost at approximately £1 000 000 per month.

- departmental budget is approximately £100 000 but an additional expenditure of £120 000 is also administered in labour costs which are allocated to individual product manufacture.

(c)   *scope and restraint*:

Function	Control	
Quality	Specification-drawings standards	Free to act in accordance with controls and to exercise some discretion on deviations
Output	Production programme Order documents and cards	Required to act
Insp. Inst.	Company quality policy	Recommend to chief inspector
Training	Training policy – quality Technical requirements	Required to act
Control	Departmental budgets Rejection returns Customer complaints	Required to act
Human relations	Agreements Legislation Safety and other policies	Required to act
Labour administration	General production programme Guidelines from Chief Inspector	Required to act

5. Relationships:

(a)   *within the company*: close and frequent association with section managers, the section leaders in quality control and with planning and distribution staff; frequent contacts with material technologies and development engineers on new products and with technical and commercial sales on specification matters; participation in the sectional planning meetings. Within the department itself there is very considerable overlap between this task and that of the quality engineer;

(b)   *outside the company*: contacts with customers and suppliers' staff on their visits here are common. Actual visits to customers or suppliers are infrequent but of substantial significance when they occur. Such visits may be overseas.

6. Skills, experience and qualifications (to be completed by the manager of the position)

Substantial experience in a practical capacity in relation to production and inspection is the usual qualification. For a relatively new person to the company, qualification to about HNC level in a relevant subject would be desirable. The job demands a familiarity with drawing conventions and the ability to read and interpret drawings and specifications of parts and products. In addition, the job requires the holder to be able to handle situations or manage people, to be able to communicate efficiently, to understand and interpret policies and instructions, e.g. manufacturing instructions, inspection procedures, safety legislation and union labour agreements, etc.

7. Other information

(a) Working conditions involve activity in all areas of the factory and certain office and development areas. Shift working is a regular requirement.

(b) Complete flexibility is necessary to cover for absence due to sickness, holiday and temporary withdrawal of individual supervisors for special tasks. When on duty outside normal day hours one supervisor is commonly responsible for the quality of all ongoing production.

(c) He is therefore often in the position of being the only individual present with authority to release material which does not conform with specifications.

8. Concurrences

Description prepared by: *Description approved by*:

_____   _____

(Analyst/Job Holder)   (Line Supervisor)
date   date

Agreed by:

_____   _____

(Job Holder/Analyst)   (Functional Head, if appropriate)
date   date

Appendix 3

Organisation Chart –

Quality Control Department

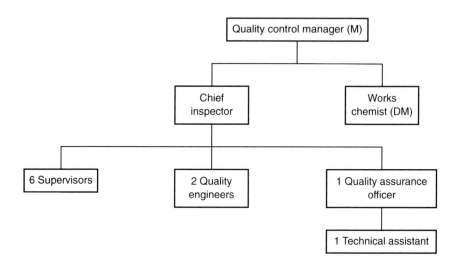

Job Description:

Supervisor (Motherwell)

[Before this job description is completed, reference should be made to the separate notes for guidance.]

1. Job title: Supervisor

Department: Quality Control
Responsible to: Chief Inspector, Motherwell

Note: an organisation chart showing the relationship of the job to other positions should also be attached (*see* Appendix 3).

2. Purpose

To supervise the examination aspects of quality control at Motherwell both as regards the direct supervision of 65 semi-skilled hourly paid examiners/patrol examiners and the quality standards achieved by production at all stages of manufacture and as despatched. In addition investigation of quality problems and submission of reports are required.

3. Main functions (accountabilities)

(a) allocate labour to jobs or jobs to labour in order to provide an efficient production service so as to assist rather than hinder the planned flow of materials and so meet planning targets;
(b) prevent, as far as possible, the production of non-standard material;
(c) control the final inspection section in order to ensure customer satisfaction within the standards laid down. The job holders will also play some part in setting the standards;
(d) advise on, and arrange for, the rectification of non-standard items where this is practicable;
(e) ensure that production is carried out according to manufacturing instructions and any necessary deviations are reported, and to assist in the development of cheaper and/or safer methods of working;
(f) run the cost centre as economically as possible and also to assist production departments in waste/reject/cost reduction;
(g) operate within Baird safety policy;
(h) promote good industrial relations.

4. Scope and dimensions

No. of employees

(a) supervision and management control
     degree of control
     management supervisor or specialist
     technical skilled manual or clerical
     routine manual or clerical
     reporting directly
     through subordinates
     indirectly controlled
(b) financial and other dimensions

Total examination budget. £285 000 p.a.
Annual cost of rejects. £200 000.

(c) scope and restraint

For direct supervision aspects the job is normally subdivided so that at any one time one supervisor has control of the final inspection force while two others on shifts control the patrol force.

For quality standard supervision aspects all supervisors are involved considerably at section managers' level with the performance of production sections as well as the inspection force itself.

Under the control of the quality manager/chief inspector and the restraints of established standards there is still considerable discretion in certain areas.

Regarding standards to be worked to, allocations of labour and solving of problems, this involves contacts with other departments and also customers and suppliers/including Glasgow.

It also involves responsibility for care and usage of inspection, and in some cases production equipment where quality is directly involved.

5. Relationships

(a) within the company: relationships are at section manager level of production – production service; planning – programs and layouts; work study – values and methods on inspection laboratory – inspection of quality control; production;
(b) outside the company: relationships involve engineering – machine/tool problems affecting quality; customers/suppliers quality engineers – relating to quality problems.

6. Skills, experience and qualifications (to be completed by manager of the position)

(a) essential: ability to read and translate into Baird terms customers' drawings and specifications. Ability to interpret manufacturing instructions and QC manuals for shop floor usage. Sufficient experience with Baird manufacturing methods is required to diagnose causes of faults before quantity production is affected and to investigate unusual features. This requires a thorough working knowledge of all types (at all operations) produced at Motherwell and some knowledge of Glasgow products and processes;

(b) desirable: general (preferably Baird) supervisory experience; knowledge of Baird planning/despatch procedures.

7. Other information

Organisation of labour is complicated by the need to balance conflicting demands from the three planning departments, together with the departmental requirements of quality control. This demands considerable flexibility of working to provide adequate cover and give good production service. Attainment of uniformity of certain arbitrary quality standards (a theoretical impossibility) is an ever present challenge. Apparently simple requests from management regarding problem solving often involve a considerable amount of effort and require consultations with a variety of departments.

Outside normal working hours the shift supervisor is the senior quality representative and is often involved in problems beyond the usual scope, e.g. involvement in laboratory testing.

Flexibility of operation between the supervisors covered by this job description is essential although there is naturally a tendency to concentrate some of the investigational aspects where experience/service of a particular individual is most suitable.

This description covers all aspects of 2380 supervision (previously covered by jobs 7035, 8067, 8068, 8046) and recognises the flexibility of staffing which can operate. There is, however, one aspect of the job (involving special investigations) which demands considerable production experience and this tends naturally to be concentrated on the man with the most suitable long service background. Even so there is considerable overlap of job content from time to time. Job 7035 which has been staffed since prior to its inception, is distributed between the incumbents of other jobs.

8. Concurrences

Description prepared by: *Description approved by*:

_____   _____

(Analyst/Job Holder)   (Line Supervisor)
date   date

Agreed by:

_____   _____

(Job Holder/Analyst)   (Functional Head, if appropriate)
date   date

Meeting between management and TSU

on Monday, 25 April 1980 (11 a.m.)

Present:

Mr A. R. McDermott – Personnel Manager
Mr A. B. Harrison – Employee Relations Manager
Mr S. A. Garner
Mr S. Kelly – Divisional Officer
Mr W. Baxter – Group Secretary
Mr N. Arnold – Glasgow
Mr L. Paterson – Motherwell

Agenda:

1. Engineering section managers' claim:
   (a) payment for covering absence of other section managers;
   (b) 13.5 per cent flexibility pay
2. Examine supervisors' claim for upgrading
3. Production section managers promoted to superintendents claim that the three section managers involved should be replaced.

1. Engineering section managers:

Mr McDermott	expressed disappointment at the attitude of these section managers. An offer has been made of £2.
Mr Kelly	we cannot accept less than £3.50 as in the agreement for 'occasional stand-in'.
Mr McDermott	the stand-in payment of £3.50 was cancelled in the agreement dated 10.6.79 when the job was upgraded. This agreement was signed by two engineering section managers, among others, on behalf of the union.
Mr Kelly	Paragraph 2.4 of the agreement dated 10.6.79 applies.
Mr McDermott	we should not have signed the document if this does not cover engineering section managers.
Mr Kelly	hourly paid engineers keep buying out flexibility. The section managers say that if it applies to them, why not us?
Mr McDermott	I will take your comments back.

2. Examine supervisors' claim:

Mr Kelly	the offer made in Mr Compton's letter was not acceptable. I agree with the company on Grade 9, the problem

is volume–manning–money. Everybody is aiming for Grade 10 – this is the best appeals procedure I have, almost every appeal is agreed for upgrading.

We have used job evaluation to get more money for our members outside the social contract.

All the problems could be accounted for in a properly used grading and appraisal scheme – taking into account the volume.

This problem can be solved by a one off payment of £304.

3. Section managers/superintendents

Agreed that a separate meeting would be held with Mr Jenkins, Mr Garner and the section managers.

Baird Ltd, Glasgow

Quality control supervisor

Joint agreed note

16 June 1980

1. Preamble

1.1 Some 18 months ago, a re-organisation of the examination structure took place. This resulted in the control of hourly paid examiners passing from quality control to production section management. It is true to say that this move never really worked, and, with hindsight, did more harm than good. The main reason for this is that quality control supervisors are really the only people qualified to effectively manage the hourly paid examiners.

1.2 For a considerable period of time now, another problem involving examination and production has been causing a great deal of concern. Rejects have been gradually increasing and are now way above the reject levels for the same period last year. The need to make a major improvement on this aspect of our business cannot be emphasised enough. The current level of rejection is not only causing us a good deal of embarrassment with our customers, but worse still, we are actually losing orders as a result. This is how critical the situation is.

1.3 One of the ways in which we can improve on this situation is to set up an effective method of supervision of production and examination. At the moment, no one is effectively managing the examiners, with the result that shoddy standards and workmanship are gradually creeping in, and general discipline is very lax.

1.4 In view of all these problems, discussions have taken place between the management and TSU officials in order to find an acceptable solution, and the following working arrangements have been agreed.

2. Working arrangements

2.1 It is agreed that the quality control supervisors will take over full control of the examiners with immediate effect. This means that the quality control supervisors will now be responsible for all aspects of the examination function, including discipline.

2.2 The quality control supervisors will work to the agreed job description. It should be understood that job descriptions are only intended to cover the main aspects of a person's job, and as such should only be used as a guide. The supervisors agree to work to this philosophy.

2.3 It is agreed that the job of 'quality control supervisor' remains Grade 9. This means that the supervisor's claim for upgrading is now dropped, and the union will not back any future claim for upgrading this job on the basis of the attached job description.

3. Spirit and intent

3.1 Much has been said recently about the very poor discipline among the examiners. This is having a bad effect on other workmen in the factory who can see low standards seemingly being accepted by the company. Also, there is no doubt that the company's reputation as a producer of top quality friction materials is no longer valid. Our customers are growing more and more concerned and, clearly, we must re-establish our position at the top as quickly as possible. This will improve confidence in our products and will help us to get new business.

3.2 The company recognises that, by taking over the examiners at this point, the supervisors will have a very difficult job to do. However, it is felt that the situation can be rectified in the next month or two, if the right attitude is applied to this task.

3.3 In recognition of this, and in answer to the claims supervisors have had with the company, it is agreed that a one-off payment will be made:

(a) once this agreement is signed the supervisors affected will be given a lump sum payment of £300 per man (subject to the usual deductions);

(b) it is clearly understood that the quality control supervisors will then be completely in charge of the examiners and will be totally committed to all aspects of discipline and good work of the examiners;

(c) it is also jointly agreed between the union and the management that although the management hold the view that the job of quality control supervisors is Grade 9, the next step in the conciliation procedure will be used in order to finalise the grading of quality control supervisors. This will be taken up by the full time officials and branch officials of the ASTMS.

4. General

4.1 We must all make every effort to minimise rejects and poor quality work, since our sales are only based on good saleable output. The company looks to its quality control department for a major contribution to this objective.

4.2 Examiners must in future be fully committed to their job.

Their standards directly influence people's livelihoods. It must be clearly understood that the quality control supervisors are now totally responsible for the examiners; they will be held accountable for ensuring that any breach of discipline is dealt with immediately.

4.3 This agreement will come into effect on Monday, 20 June 1980.

Signed on behalf of the   Signed on behalf of the union
management

_____   _____

_____   _____

_____   _____

Dated: _____   Dated: _____

Questions

1 Do you think that the job descriptions give enough information to enable a judgment to be formed regarding the relative levels of job?
2 Has management acted in a considerate manner throughout the negotiations?
3 How would you grade these jobs and what criteria would you use?

Arbitration between
HARLEQUIN BOTTLERS LTD
and
SOFT DRINK MANUFACTURERS AND
DISTRIBUTORS TRADE UNION
(in respect of unfair dismissal)

Terms of reference

The terms of reference agreed by both parties were:

> 'To consider the appeal by Mr Bob Parsons against his dismissal from the company.'

Documentation

The arbitrator received a statement of the case from both the company and the appellant supported by the union. Both parties had received and studied each other's submissions.

Background to the dispute

Mr Bob Parsons is employed by Harlequin Bottlers as a line worker in the bottling plant at Derby Road, Hull. He was on sick leave from 28 March to 30 September with chest wall strain. He reported for work on 1 October and then took annual leave from 11 October to 2 November. On 5 November he returned to work and spent the day sighting bottles for 'splits', i.e. cracks. The following day Mr Parsons was asked to work on 'big bottles' which involves lifting crates of full bottles on to palletts. He refused the work and after some discussion with the shift manager was suspended on full pay.

The disciplinary procedure was followed through to dismissal which was confirmed on 30 November. An internal appeal followed on 10 January which confirmed the dismissal decision. The procedure allows a final appeal with an independent arbitrator and the union advised Mr Parsons to go to final appeal in an attempt to regain his job.

THE UNION CASE FOR THE ARBITRATOR

The Soft Drinks Manufacturers and Distributors Trade Union

To: the arbitrator

Union House
9 Commercial Street
Hull

Dear Sir

Mr Bob Parsons has been a loyal and devoted worker at Harlequin Bottlers for 12 years. His wife, Doreen, has also worked for the company for many years until she had an accident at work. Some bottles were smashed in the machine and Mrs Parsons cut her arm very badly. Her compensation was very poor despite the fact that she now has a numb thumb very often and cannot hold things.

Although he is now 57 and there are many younger men on the line Vic Friar, the Shift Manager, repeatedly asked Bill to work the big bottles. Because of this Bob twisted his back and had to go to the doctor who gave him certificates for 6 months.

When he went back to work Mr Friar victimised him again by calling him 'Grandad' and 'Sissy'. On the 6 November Mr Friar asked him to work the big bottles which Bob refused. He then called Bob a 'bloody timewaster', a 'lead swinger' and worse. That was the reason Bob Parsons refused the job he was told to do.

If he was re-instated he could easily do all the jobs in the factory except the big bottles. He would be very willing to do this but he does not want to work with Vic Friar any more.

We ask you to uphold his appeal.

Yours sincerely

Terry Buller
SDMDTU Official

THE COMPANY CASE FOR THE ARBITRATOR

To: the arbitrator:

Harlequin Bottlers
Derby Road
Hull

Dear Sir

Mr R. Parsons — Bottling Line

Mr Parsons has worked for this company for several years and is regarded as a competent bottling line worker. He is experienced in loading, sighting, washing, packing and checking on both small and large bottle lines.

After six months sick leave with back strain Mr Parsons returned to work as fully fit on the 1 October with a recommendation that he have light duties for two weeks. This request was adhered to.

On 6 November he was asked to work on the big bottle line as packer and refused. He was then offered lighter work sighting bottles for cracks by the shift manager. This he also refused. He was again offered this light work in the presence of the Shop Steward and refused despite the shop steward's advice to accept. Mr Parsons was immediately suspended according to procedure.

At the subsequent hearing Mr Parsons was dismissed from the company. He appealed and was turned down. He has now invoked the final stage of the appeal with an independent arbitrator.

We trust that you will agree that the company has acted appropriately and that you will dismiss the appeal.

R. A. Hutchinson
General Manager

ASSOCIATED DOCUMENTS

These documents are common to both the union and the employers' cases

Harlequin Bottlers Ltd

Notes regarding the meeting with R. Parsons on 6 November 1990

At 2.10 p.m. approximately, R. Parsons came to the shift manager's office. He had been allocated to the big bottles unit and he did not want to work on that unit. He did not think the unit was safe, his side was hurting and he did not want to do any lifting. R. Parsons said that the company doctor had given him 'light duties'.

V. Friar then left R. Parsons and went into the factory (shift) manager's office, to check the wording of the doctor's report with Helen.

'Following hospital treatment, medical condition has settled. It would be helpful to Mr Parsons if heavy lifting be avoided for two weeks.' (Dated 26 September)

V. Friar and Ann Welcome (Supervisor) offered R. Parsons sighting on big bottles, which would not involve lifting the full containers. R. Parsons would not work on the big bottle unit. He asked 'What do I do now?' and was sent to see his Shop Steward, Harry Black.

R. Parsons returned, saying he wanted a meeting with V. Friar and Harry Black. This was immediately arranged. In this meeting R. Parsons again expressed concern at the safety of the big bottle unit (his wife had had an accident when working there). V. Friar explained:

1. that the recent modifications had been approved by the factory inspector, and
2. that the factory inspector was satisfied and a copy of his letter was with the union (H. Black).

V. Friar asked R. Parsons in the presence of his shop steward to work on the big bottles unit. R Parsons replied that he did not want to, for safety and lifting reasons. R. Parsons currently has no sick pay entitlement and has used all this year's holiday entitlement.

V. Friar stated that R. Parsons, having clocked in, had made himself available for work. He had not complained previously. He had not asked for an appointment to see the company doctor. As R. Parsons was fit for work, he should go sighting on the big bottle unit. R. Parsons refused, saying he would not work on the big bottles unit. His shop steward advised him to work, adding that the option was his and no one could make him do it, if he did not want to. H. Black added that he could not see any argument to support. R. Parsons again refused.

V. Friar outlined that R. Parsons may be endangering his employment by refusing a 'reasonable request'. R. Parsons again refused.

V. Friar suspended R. Parsons on pay, pending a meeting. He was instructed to clock out and leave the site.

R. Parsons clocked out at 3 p.m.

V. Friar
Shift Manager

Harlequin Bottlers Ltd
Disciplinary notice

From: Vic Friar

Date: 8 November 1990

To: R. Parsons

cc: Personal File
      H. Black (Shop Steward)

re: Incident on 6 November

I confirm that following the incident on Tuesday 6 November, you are suspended on 'full average pay', in accordance with the Harlequin disciplinary procedures.

I hope to arrange a disciplinary hearing of your case for early next week, subject to the availability of senior management.

If you have any queries with regard to the above matter or your current circumstances, please do not hesitate to contact either myself or your shop steward through the usual channels.

Vic Friar
Shift Manager

Disciplinary meeting

(29 November 1990)

Present:

Mr V. Friar
Mr V. Youngson
Mr R. Parsons
Mr H. Black

V. Friar called the meeting to further review the disciplinary case arising from the incident on the 6 November.

V. Friar opened the meeting by reading the notes which summarised the events of 6 November.

R. Parsons	On Monday (5 November) I was put on a light job – standing bottles on Line 4. If I had known I would be working on big bottles on the Tuesday, I would have gone 'sick'. After the suspension, I went to the doctor and was given a certificate for two weeks, if I wanted to use it.
V. Friar	Why, if your side was hurting, did you report for work on the Monday?'
R. Parsons	I had no sick pay left, and also thought I would have the same job on Tuesday that I had on Monday.
V. Friar	What is your current state of health?
R. Parsons	I have rested for three weeks and feel better now. I have worked big bottles for six and a half years, and have never refused big bottles before. My doctor warned me about my condition – like an elastic band – with twisting and bending it could 'go' at any time.
V. Friar	If you were put on big bottles tomorrow, would you be fit to work?
R. Parsons	Yes

Adjournment

Reconvene

V. Friar	I informed R. Parsons and H. Black that after further consideration, it is my recommendation to dismiss R. Parsons. A hearing with John Bailey, Works Manager, is arranged for 11 a.m. on Friday 30 November. R. Parsons is to arrive at 10 a.m., when all relevant papers will be available for review with H. Black.

Harlequin Bottlers Ltd

Memorandum

From: Vic Friar   To: Mr John Bailey
                                                            Works Manager

Date: 29 November 1990

re: R. Parsons

Following a full investigation of the disciplinary case, I find that Mr R. Parsons has committed gross misconduct in refusing to carry out a reasonable management instruction.

I confirm my earlier verbal recommendation to dismiss Mr Parsons.

A meeting has been arranged for 11 a.m. on Friday 30 November.

Vic Friar
Shift Manager

Disciplinary communication

From: Vic Friar   To   R. Parsons

Date: 29 November 1990   cc: Personnel File
                                                            H. Black

re: Dismissal hearing

The dismissal hearing is arranged for 11 a.m. on Friday 30 November. Your shop steward will be available prior to the case, to help you prepare.

Vic Friar
Shift Manager

Dismissal hearing – 30 November 1990

Present:

J. Bailey – Works Manager
V. Friar – Shift Manager
H. Black – Shop Steward
R. Parsons –Technical Operator

Mr Bailey checked through the notes:

Dismissal hearing: VF–RP
VF–JB re: RP
Notes: re: meeting 6 November
Disciplinary meeting:

J. Bailey	Asked V. Friar to relate the events.
R. Parsons	Company doctor 26th (Rec. ret. 1 October) – light duties for two weeks. Half way through 2nd week, began sighting on L3, booked two weeks' holidays commencing 22 October.
	2nd week (w/c 8/10) ribs hurting. Did not mention this to anybody – worried that it would start again. Then toothache (week's holiday) started 15/10. Returned 5/11 – side still hurting, on L4 combiner. Assumed because not told anything, would be there on Tuesday. Heard would be on big bottles Tuesday.
J. Bailey	What is the difference?
R. Parsons	Not knowing job, didn't want lengthy lay-off.
J. Bailey	Who told you...?
R. Parsons	John (L4)(withheld names)
	If not going on there, assumed someone would tell me. Caused in the first place by lifting bins.
J. Bailey	Did you report it?
R. Parsons	I did not report it, no, but Fred Armstrong knows about it.
	Mentioned safety ...
	Cracked ribs started it ...
	No objection to going on big bottles ...
J. Bailey	What job?
R. Parsons	Sighting.
J. Bailey	Is this considered 'heavy'?
R. Parsons	I consider it 'heavy'.
	Asked to see company doctor but V. Friar said 'too late'.
J. Bailey	Do you know the job?

R. Parsons	Yes.
	(J. Bailey read through the letter)
R. Parsons	Company doctor said if not cured, come back and see me.
J. Bailey	Did you?
R. Parsons	With sick pay... the doctor might put me off again.
J. Bailey	Did V. Friar's explanation of the modifications and the factory inspector's letter not satisfy you of the safety?
R. Parsons	No.
J. Bailey	Why not?
R. Parsons	Because of an accident to a personal friend.
J. Bailey	It seems to me that your refusal is based on the unit being an unsafe place to work.
R. Parsons	Yes.
J. Bailey	Your refusal was based on safety?
R. Parsons	Yes at that time.
J. Bailey	(Explained refusal can only be given at a moment in time)
R. Parsons	Confused over sighting full or empty.
J. Bailey	Asked for Ann Wellcome and left meeting.
J. Bailey	How many work on the big bottles unit normally?
A. Wellcome	Four.
J. Bailey	How many were working on that day?
A. Wellcome	Three.
J. Bailey	What job was R. Parsons asked to do?
A. Wellcome	Sighting.
J. Bailey	Was that full or empty sighting?
A. Wellcome	Full.
J. Bailey	Did he have to push them down the conveyor?
A. Wellcome	No, lifting of full crates.
J. Bailey	Confusion over job – sighting and passing round the line?
R. Parsons	Who says I was fit for work?
J. Bailey	You, by clocking in.
R. Parsons	If I had known what Mr Friar wanted, I would have worked on the unit. I have no objections with that.
	After I was suspended, I went to see my own doctor, who examined me and said that, in his opinion, I was not fit for work. I was given a doctor's note.
J. Bailey	I don't consider either job to be 'heavy'. You said you would not work on the big bottles unit for safety reasons. You were given 'light duties' but your refusal came without your having looked at the job's requirements.
	If your refusal was based on health, you should have taken Mr Friar with you to the unit, and shown him the problem.

At yesterday's meeting, you did not mention safety. It seems to me that you have raised this as an afterthought.

Reviewed yesterday's meeting.

Have you anything else to say?

R. Parsons	The Doctor asked me to see if 'light duties' could be arranged. I also emphasise that if I had known – I would have had no objections.
J. Bailey	It was explained to you that your refusal could endanger your job. Why did you not go and see the job? You could have been to see personnel, your shop steward or the doctor, but you did not. Instead, you chose the rough-shod route.

Although there was some confusion on the day it was not a 'heavy' job.

You emphasised on two occasions that you would not work on the unit, because you considered it to be unsafe. You did not take Mr Friar to the unit to show him the problem.

R. Parsons	Satisfied with the safety.
J. Bailey	Then, if Mr Friar was satisfied with the safety, why did you refuse? Why was there no mention of safety yesterday? Is it not true you thought the unit was not safe?
R. Parsons	Yes, I did.
J. Bailey	Why did you then express safety as an issue?
R. Parsons	Why did Mr Friar ask if I was fit for work? (yesterday)
V. Friar	I was enquiring about his current state of health.
R. Parsons	If I had seen the company doctor and he had told me two more weeks 'light duties', then I would have worked on the unit.
	Why was I suspended for three weeks, but was not allowed to do 'light duties'?
V. Friar	I explained that three days were required by the agreement and that Mr Bailey was off-site for eight days.
J. Bailey	You heard by the 'grapevine' that you would be on the big bottles unit, on Monday. Why did you not go and see somebody and ask about it then?
R. Parsons	Not sure who the supervisor was. Is it still Fred Armstrong?
J. Bailey	Why did you not ask anybody?
R. Parsons	I don't listen to rumours.
J. Bailey	You were justified to ask.
R. Parsons	Yes, but not that sort of bloke.
J. Bailey	But you refused.

R. Parsons	Not that sort of bloke.
J. Bailey	Are there any more questions you want to ask, or you want me to ask?
H. Black	I am satisfied that all the points have been covered.

J. Bailey left the meeting at 12.27 p.m.

The meeting resumed at 12.42 p.m.

J. Bailey

The first request was reasonable. It would be reasonable to challenge because you were off sick when there was a nasty accident.

The manager explained and you agree: changes to the unit and the factory inspector's letter.

You also mentioned your back/side hurting. You are entitled to 'light duties', true, but due to the time that has lapsed, and the fact that you have not visited the doctor, this is now out of date.

The manager knew your 'light duties' period had lapsed. However, 'light duties' were suggested to you. You did not challenge whether the job was 'light' or not and I accept that there was some confusion over the exact job. However, you should have taken it further and found out exactly what was required of you.

After the explanation given by your manager, you mentioned safety again.

Considering your knowledge of plant and the job the manager offered, I believe that I will uphold the manager's recommendation to dismiss you for not carrying out a reasonable request.

You will have an opportunity to discuss pay situations with a manager and shop steward.

You were aware of the consequences when you decided to take this option.

You are dismissed from Harlequin, but you do have rights. As per the 'Blue Book', you have five days to appeal.

R. Parsons	I am going to appeal. Is this so serious – to go from a first written warning?
J. Bailey	Yes, gross misconduct and gross negligence warrant dismissal.

I suggest R. Parsons discuss the situation with H. Black.

Harlequin Bottlers Ltd

Recorded delivery

Derby Road
Hull
3 December 1990

R. Parsons
5 Hindley Street
Hull

Dear Mr Parsons

I confirm my conclusion reached at the dismissal hearing held in my office on Friday 30 November, when I informed you that you were immediately dismissed from the employment of Harlequin Bottlers for gross misconduct.

The dismissal resulted from your refusing to carry out a reasonable request asked of you by your manager to work on the big bottles unit on the 6 November.

Your initial refusal was based on the fact that the work you were asked to carry out was unsafe, and further to this you were concerned as to your health. Your manager took both points into consideration, firstly by explaining the safety precautions which had recently been put into place and, secondly, by ensuring the work involved only light duties.

Even after these explanations you continued to refuse to carry out the request to work. Further to this you were advised to do the work in question by your shop steward (Mr Harry Black). You continued to refuse.

During the hearing you stated that the company doctor suggested you be given light duties for two weeks on your return to work after 26 weeks' sickness, although you returned to work on 1 October, some five weeks before your refusal to carry out your manager's request to work the big bottles unit. Therefore, it was considerate of your manager to continue to give you light duties, but you still refused to do the work.

All points raised by yourself and your shop steward were taken into account. The conclusion reached was based on the fact that you had ample opportunity to reconsider the situation after explanations had been given, and you were amply warned of the consequence of your refusal to carry out a reasonable request asked of you by your manager. Further to this you continued to refuse to take the advice given by your shop steward which would have alleviated the situation.

The hearing was held in accordance with the Harlequin disciplinary procedure. You were represented by your SDMDTU shop steward. Your right to appeal against the decision of the hearing was explained to you where the procedure states that if you decide to appeal you must do so in writing within five working days of the dismissal taking effect.

Yours sincerely

J. Bailey
Works Manager

Appeal against dismissal

R. Parsons
5 Hindley Street
Hull
3 December 1990

Dear Mr Bailey

I am appealing against the decision made at the meeting on Friday 30 November of dismissal for 'gross misconduct' as I find this totally unacceptable. The reasons I am appealing are:

1. I told the shift manager that I considered myself myself not fit enough to work on big bottles, and could I see the company doctor so that he could decide whether I was fit for work or not, and I was refused this and told it was too late for that. I told him that I had a 'lot of pain' in my side, and couldn't do any bending, lifting or twisting, and if I worked on this job it would probably do 'damage', and I had no sick pay left and I would be off work for a long while again. I feel that the company doctor should have made the decision whether I was fit for work, not the shift manager.
2. I was refused the chance to see the company doctor, but I feel that I should have been sent to see him, not have had to ask.

3. After not being allowed the chance to see the company doctor, and possibly have been given more light duties or time off by him, I was then suspended for three weeks and two days, waiting for a hearing. Having been given all this time to recover, which is all I wanted in the first place. I am now fully fit after this rest.

4. Also I went to my own doctor on Tuesday night 6 November, which was the day I was suspended, and he examined me and told me 'no way should I have been at work at all' and gave me a 'medical certificate' for two weeks off work. I am totally convinced that the company doctor would have done exactly the same, and I am therefore lodging a 'failure to agree' on the decision and request another hearing, hoping you can arrange this. Finally I have enclosed a 'photo copy' of my medical certificate for you to look at.

Yours sincerely

R. Parsons

Harlequin Bottlers Ltd

Appeal against dismissal – R. Parsons: 10 January 1991

Present:

Alan Marshall – General Manager
John Bailey – Works Manager
Fiona Simmons – HR Manager
R. Parsons – Appellant
D. Carter – Shop Steward
H. Black – Shop Steward
T. Buller – SDMDTU–Full time official

John Bailey asked if the absence of Vic Friar due to holiday was acceptable and apologised for the delay in setting up the appeal which was due to Christmas holidays.

John Bailey opened proceedings and re-stated the facts of the case which briefly were:

R. Parsons returned from holiday after prolonged sickness absence on 5 November. Chest strain had caused him to be off during periods 14–39 (March–October).

He had returned to work 1 October and worked for eight days. He then needed to take a holiday as he had no sick pay left and he had had problems with toothache. He returned after his holiday.

He had had a medical with the company doctor on 26 September before his return. He was advised that he was fit to work but to have light duties on his return for two weeks. This note had expired several weeks before he returned to work after holiday, on 5 November. However, he was still given light duties, sighting splits on Line 4.

On the 6 November he was working late shift, clocked in at 2 p.m., as fit, and was asked to work on the big bottles. He refused because he felt there were safety problems on the big bottles.

There had been improvements on big bottles safety while Bob Parsons was off sick; also the factory inspector had been involved and had written a letter. Vic Friar explained all this to Bob Parsons who had previously worked for six years on big bottles. Bob Parsons then refused to work on the big bottles. He was given ample opportunity to reconsider his decision. His steward H. Black told him to work. Bob Parsons went to his own doctor the evening of the 6th to get a medical note but this was not relevant. There are three recorded refusals to work. After his meeting with Vic Friar he was suspended pending a disciplinary meeting. There was a meeting arranged with Mrs Youngson and Vic Friar to discuss the situation before the dismissal hearing and when asked if he would work on big bottles if fit to work, he said 'Yes'.

At the dismissal hearing John Bailey went out of his way to ensure the job Bob Parsons was asked to do was light work. It was. John Bailey went and checked for himself. At the dismissal hearing Bob Parsons still refused to work so he was dismissed.

T. Buller opened the basis appeal on two counts:

1. Was the instruction to work on big bottles reasonable in the circumstances? and following on,
2. Was the decision to dismiss Bob Parsons reasonable in the circumstances?

T. Buller (SDMTDU) concurred that Bob Parsons's reaction not to work was wrong, and that he should have worked under protest. He stated that it was an injury at work which resulted in chest problems from cracked ribs five years ago. This was not reported. The facts were as follows:

When Bob Parsons returned from sick leave he took holiday as he had no sick pay left. He had toothache.

He returned on 5 November and sighted splits on Line 4 which involved light duties. He was asked to work on big bottles on the 6th. He was concerned about safety and also thought the job was heavy and involved lifting and bending. He felt that management did not communicate that it was light work. He thought he was asked to sight big bottles for cracks, and this involved twisting and bending. The job was actually sorting empty bottles which is light work. He thought the job was in the middle of the line. Too much twisting would set his back off at any time.

Bob Parsons asked why he wasn't allowed to see the company doctor on the 6th to check out his health. He didn't have any sick pay left, so didn't want to be laid off for a long time. Vic Friar had told him it was too late to see a doctor.

Alan Marshall (General Manager) asked R. Parsons if it was correct that at the meeting with Vic Friar he refused to work on big bottles because of safety. R. Parsons agreed. A. Marshall then asked R. Parsons if it was correct that at the disciplinary meeting R. Parsons said he would work on big bottles if he was fit. R. Parsons said that after three weeks' rest he was fit and that was why he said 'Yes'.

Bob Parsons said he was concerned about 'personal' safety and this meant his health. He complained that he was not told he would be moved off Line 4 to big bottles on the 6th. He said he should have been told the day before, not on Tuesday when he turned up for work. He was worried about his health, said his back could go at any time, that it was like a 'rubber band'. Alan Marshall asked why he had reported fit for work at 2 p.m. then. Bob Parsons said he had no sick pay left. Alan Marshall said it was a fair assumption by Vic Friar if he reported for work at 2 p.m. that he was fit. Nevertheless, he was still offered light duties on the big bottles. He was asked what job he did before his extended period of sick leave. He did the stacking job on Line 2. Bob Parsons complained that the job had not been kept open for him over the seven month period he was sick (this job is much heavier than Line 4 sighting on big bottles and involves lifting crates).

T. Buller and Bob Parsons accepted that he reacted wrongly and should have worked under protest. But wasn't the decision to dismiss unreasonable considering his 12 year's service? He didn't understand the job he was offered. Lesser discipline would have been more appropriate. T. Buller was concerned over the three and a half week suspension (John Bailey had already apologised over holidays causing delay). T. Buller was also concerned that Bob Parsons was not told there was a recommendation to dismiss him and communications had been poor. John Bailey said Bob Parsons knew about the recommendation to dismiss him and that there was a typing omission on the dismissal hearing notification. He was well aware, as told at the disciplinary meeting. Alan Marshall asked why if Bob Parsons's ribs were hurting did he report for work at 2 p.m. if his major concern was his health? Why did he say 'Yes' when asked if fit to work by V. Friar at the second meeting? Bob Parsons then said his ribs could go at any time. He felt the big bottles job was not safe for his ribs. He said 'You can't tell when it is going to start'. But at the meeting he said 'Yes' because his ribs were OK after the rest from three weeks' suspension.

The meeting was then adjourned for Alan Marshall to make a decision. The meeting re-convened and Alan Marshall read the following statement after asking if Fiona Simmons could be excused.

The basis of appeal concerns:

1. Was the instruction reasonable in the circumstances?
2. Was the decision to dismiss reasonable in the circumstances?

He reported for work as fit. His light duty medical advice expired in October some weeks prior. There has been some confusion over which job was concerned. Nevertheless, an experienced manager judged that the sighting job or sorting job is light work albeit that sighting splits is lighter. The instruction was reasonable.

Was Bob Parsons's attitude reasonable and genuine? He did not listen to advice from the steward to take this opportunity to look at the job which undoubtedly would have cleared up any confusion. He is inconsistent in saying today that he accepted on the 6 November that there was not a safety issue, whereas on 30 November at the disciplinary meeting he said that Vic Friar's explanation of the modifications and factory inspector's letter did not satisfy him.

As to his medical reason for not doing the job, Mr Parsons says today he was in pain on 5 November and yet was unhappy that he was not on the stacking job on Line 2 which is heavier than the big bottles job. The pain he states is OK when rested and yet on 2nd day of working, 6 November, he was concerned that the big bottles job may at any time in the shift aggravate the complaint. On the 29th after his three week suspension he says he would now be all right to do the job. I find Mr Parsons's explanation inconsistent and varying according to the circumstances over this period.

I, therefore, cannot accept the view his attitude was reasonable and genuine to this instruction particularly in view of the opportunity to go and look at the job.

To the question was the decision to dismiss reasonable in the circumstances, my view on this is very much tied in to the reasons why I see the instruction as reasonable and Mr Parsons's attitude was not reasonable. I, therefore, agree that he committed gross misconduct.

Taking account of his service and his current disciplinary record I find it difficult to see how management discretion could have been applied not to dismiss taking account of all the circumstances.

I, therefore, uphold the dismissal decision and the dismissal is effective as of today, 10 January. In accordance with Harlequin procedures Mr Parsons has the right of appeal to higher authority than me, and he should put such in writing in five working days. We will write to him giving the outcome of this appeal and relevant pay details.

R. Parsons
5 Hindley Street
Hull   14 January 1991

Dear Mr Parsons

I confirm my decision reached at the appeal hearing held in J. Bailey's office on Thursday 10 January, when I informed you that I upheld the dismissal decision reached by Mr Bailey on 30 November.

The basis of your appeal was put forward by T. Buller, SDMDTU, in accordance with Harlequin disciplinary procedures. The basis was:

1. Was the instruction (to work on big bottles) reasonable in the circumstances?
2. Was the decision to dismiss reasonable in the circumstances?

Point 1.

You reported for work fit on 6 November. The medical certificate advising light duties had expired some weeks previously in October, yet you were still offered light duties by your manager. There has been some confusion over which job you were asked to do; nevertheless, an experienced senior manager judged that whether it was sighting or sorting on big bottles, both were light duties. Sighting splits is lighter, but in any case you were not asked to do heavy work.

The instruction was therefore reasonable in the circumstances.

I question whether your attitude was reasonable and genuine. You did not listen to advice from your own shop steward to take the opportunity to look at the job which undoubtedly would have cleared up any confusion.

You are inconsistent on the safety issue. At the appeal hearing you stated that on 6 November you accepted there was not a safety issue, whereas you stated at the dismissal hearing on 30 November that you were not satisfied by V. Friar's explanations of the modification on big bottles and the factory inspector's letter.

As to your medical reason for not doing the job, you stated at the appeal that you were in pain on 5 November and yet you were unhappy that you were not back on the stacking job on Line 2, which is heavier than the big bottles job. You stated that the pain is all right when you have rested and yet on the 6 November, the second day of working after your holiday, you were concerned that the big bottle job may aggravate your complaint at any time in the shift.

On 29 November, after three weeks' suspension, you stated you would be all right to do the job now.

I find your explanations inconsistent and vary according to the circumstances over this period.

I therefore cannot accept that your attitude was reasonable and genuine to this instruction, particularly in view of the opportunity to look at the job.

Point 2.

My decision on this is very much allied to the reasons why I viewed the instruction as reasonable and your attitude as not reasonable. I therefore agree with the previous decision that you committed gross misconduct. Taking into account your service, current disciplinary record and all the circumstances, I find it difficult to see how management discretion could have been applied not to dismiss you.

I therefore have decided to uphold the dismissal decision and the dismissal is effective as of 10 January. You will receive any monies due to you in the normal way.

This appeal was heard in accordance with Harlequin disciplinary procedures and you were represented by both shop stewards and the local SDMDTU official.

It was explained to you that you now have the right to appeal to a higher authority than me and should put such request in writing within five working days of the appeal hearing.

Yours sincerely

A. Marshall
General Manager

T. Buller
SDMDTU
Union House
9 Commercial Street
Hull   11 February 1991

Dear Mr Buller

re: R. Parsons

This is to confirm my telephone call to your office when I advised that Mr Parsons's appeal will be heard in the works manager's office at 2.00 p.m. on Monday 25 February.

I look forward to seeing you at that time.

Yours sincerely

Fiona Simmons
Human Resources Manager

R. Parsons
5 Hindley Street
Hull   11 February 1991

Dear Mr Parsons

This letter is to confirm that your appeal will be held here on Monday 25 February at 2.00 p.m. in the works manager's office.

The company director in attendance to hear the appeal will be Mr A. R. Knightley and an independent ACAS arbitrator will also be present.

We look forward to seeing you on that date.

Yours sincerely

Fiona Simmons
Human Resources Manager

Harlequin Bottlers Ltd

Disciplinary procedure

The aim of this disciplinary procedure is to bring about corrective action where an employee's conduct or job performance falls below acceptable standards.

For the first occurrence of minor offences such as lateness or minor errors in work, informal verbal warnings should be given by the employee's supervisor or immediate manager so that corrective action can be taken without recourse to the formal procedure. However, where minor offences continue or a more serious offence is committed then the following formal procedure will be followed.

Disciplinary procedure

1.1 **Formal verbal warning**: for minor offences this will be given by the employee's supervisor, immediate manager or departmental manager and confirmed in writing as a verbal warning.

1.2 **Written warning**: for more serious offences, lack of sustained improvement in previous offences for which the employee has received a formal verbal warning or the commitment of further or other offences, this will be given by the employee's immediate manager.

1.3 **Final written warning**: for offences of serious misconduct, lack of sustained improvement in previous offence for which the employee has received a written warning or the commitment of further or other offences, this will be given by the employee's immediate manager or departmental manager. The employee will be informed that the commitment of another offence may lead to dismissal.

1.4 An employee subject to any formal disciplinary interview will:
  (a) be informed prior to the hearing of the complaint against him with the time and place of the hearing confirmed in writing;
  (b) have the right to be accompanied by his shop steward or fellow employee of his choice;
  (c) be given the opportunity to state his case;
  (d) receive written confirmation of the disciplinary interview and where appropriate a time by which an improvement in performance or behaviour is expected.

  In all cases of formal disciplinary action the appropriate shop steward will be informed that action is being taken.

1.5 **Records**
  Minor offences: Minor offences for which a formal verbal warning has been given will be removed from the individual's record card by

his immediate manager after a time of six months has elapsed from the date that the verbal warning was given, provided no further warnings have been given.

Serious offences: Disciplinary warnings for serious offences will be removed from the individual's record card after two years has elapsed from the date that the warning was given, provided no further warnings have been given.

2. Procedure for dismissal

2.1 Circumstances warranting dismissal

Dismissal decisions for disciplinary reasons arise from any of the following situations:

2.1.1 Failure to meet or sustain the required standard of conduct or performance at work when already having received a final warning.

2.1.2 Misconduct warranting a disciplinary warning when already having received a final warning.

2.1.3 Gross misconduct.

3. Dismissal

An employee concerned in circumstances warranting dismissal is entitled to a full and fair hearing before any decision to dismiss. Such a hearing will take place only after a comprehensive investigation by the immediate manager, including an interview.

3.1 Essential requirements during investigation preparatory to the dismissal hearing are:

(a) notification of the position to the employee concerned and the employee's shop steward;

(b) investigation of all the relevant facts, including the statements of witnesses and allowing adequate time;

(c) documents or extracts which will be used at the hearing made available to the employee;

(d) an interview between the immediate manager and the employee, together with the shop steward or fellow employee;

(e) confirmation of a recommendation to dismiss together with the principle reason(s);

(f) a management decision to suspend the employee from normal duties if warranted, pending the investigation and interview. Suspension will attract full average pay, to the conclusion of the first appeal.

3.2 The dismissal hearing determines whether a recommendation to dismiss should be confirmed.

Essential requirements for a proper hearing are:

(a) the authorised senior manager (schedule refers) conducts proceedings and having heard from all concerned and taking into account any mitigating circumstances will decide either to accept or reject the recommendations to dismiss;

(b) it takes place as soon as possible but not earlier than three working days following a recommendation to dismiss to allow proper preparation;

(c) the employees can be represented by a fellow employee or shop steward and/or the regional (factory) steward. The full time trade union officer may attend at trade union request;

(d) if the employee concerned is a shop steward, the full time trade union officer must be in attendance at the dismissal hearing;

(e) the hearing will receive a presentation of the facts supported by the evidence and the reasons for the dismissal recommendation, normally given by the recommending manager with any witnesses;

(f) it will equally receive the employee's explanation and any additional facts relevant to the hearing together with any further witnesses.

3.3 A dismissed employee will receive a written statement from the senior manager containing the reason for dismissal, the effective date, and the right of appeal, with a copy to the employee's shop steward.

4. First appeal

4.1 A dismissed employee who decides to appeal must notify his manager in writing within five working days of the dismissal.

4.2 An appeal against dismissal will be heard by an employee's director.

(a) attendance at the appeal will be those present at the dismissal hearing with a trade union full time officer representing the dismissed employee;

(b) Harlequin Bottlers personnel department provides administration support and advice to the hearing on agreements procedure and Harlequin Bottlers practice;

(c) the director will decide either to accept or to reject the appeal taking account of all the material facts and circumstances presented at the dismissal hearing.

4.3 If the appeal is rejected dismissal takes effect on conclusion of the appeal hearing. The employee will be notified in writing together with relevant details on pay.

4.4 An employee so dismissed who decides to appeal must notify his director in writing stating his reasons within five working days of dismissal.

Second appeal

4.5   The second appeal hearing will be heard by the Harlequin Bottlers managing director or, in his absence, a Harlequin Bottlers director, together with an independent arbitrator acceptable to both sides.

(a)   the appeal hearing will be heard as soon as possible but within six weeks of receipt of the appeal unless mutually agreed otherwise;

(b)   attendance at this appeal hearing will be those present at the first appeal hearing, except the director hearing the first appeal;

(c)   the director and the independent arbitrator will decide either to accept or reject the appeal, taking account of all the material facts and circumstances presented at the dismissal hearing.

4.6   If the appeal is upheld the employee will be reinstated with retro-spective payments to the date of dismissal.

4.7   The outcome of the appeal will be notified in writing to the employee with a copy to the employee's shop steward, and the procedure concludes at this point.

Questions

1   Did the company follow the agreed disciplinary procedure properly?

2   Did Mr Parsons receive sufficient support when carrying through his appeal?

3   What decisions would you have reached?

Arbitration between

ROWLANDS ENGINEERING LTD

and

the CONSTRUCTION WORKERS UNION
(management staff)

(in respect of resident engineers following a restructuring of the company)

Terms of reference

'To consider and determine the grading of the posts occupied by W. Arnold and J. Peters currently resident engineers on Grade 9.'

Background to the dispute

Rowlands Engineering Ltd is a medium sized civil engineering company specialising in the design and construction of supermarkets. The company provides a full design and construction service on a turnkey basis to many clients but the present case relates to the building of supermarkets and the control of a contract with subcontractors.

The engineering department was restructured three years ago to enable it to cope with the increasing volume of projects contained in the capital works programme. Each project carried out within the engineering department was managed from inception, throughout the whole range of activities, through to completion by a project engineer. The project engineers were responsible to a group engineer. The majority of design was carried out in-house and the supervision of the construction contracts was provided by a team of permanent in-house resident engineers and clerks of works supplemented from time to time with appropriate temporary staff. Each civil engineering contract was carried out under the supervision of a nominated 'engineer' who was supported on site by the resident engineers and clerks of works. The nominated 'engineer' was normally a group engineer but after the restructuring could have been a principal engineer.

The appellants, Mr Arnold and Mr Peters, are employed as resident engineers. Their claim is for re-grading from Grade 9 to Grade 10 on the basis of increased duties and responsibilities following the restructuring. In particular the claim concerns the work done by these two resident engineers during the building of Blagdon supermarket where the nature of the contracts they supervised was, they claim, markedly changed compared with previous practice.

The claim for re-grading has followed the procedures laid down by the company and culminated in a grading appeal hearing held on 11 May. At this hearing the panel reached a 'failure to agree' but made an ex gratia payment of £1500 to each appellant. The internal procedures having been exhausted the dispute was referred to independent arbitration. Both sides have exchanged written documentation with agreed common 'information' on job descriptions.

THE TRADE UNION STATEMENT OF CASE

Construction Workers Union

CWU House
Haymarket
Leicester

To: arbitration panel   8 November

Dear Sirs

1. Mr Arnold and Mr Peters are employed by Rowlands Engineering Ltd as resident engineers in the company's head office. Their applications for re-grading are attached as associated documents. The job description for their post is also attached.
2. At a grading appeal hearing on 11 May the panel reached a 'failure to agree' but made an ex gratia payment to each appellant of £1500. A copy of the appeals panel decision is also attached.
3. The appellants claim is one of increased duties and responsibilities predicated upon:
    (a) co-ordination of major projects on one site;
    (b) negotiating with major contractors to solve boundary/access problems;
    (c) management of staff; and
    (d) greatly increased involvement and responsibility with regard to safety.

4. Prior to the commencement of Blagdon supermarket, practice was such that a resident engineer supervised one major contract at one time. In this situation the contractor's agent was responsible for site safety and for the co-ordination of all activities on the site. The resident engineers' involvement used to be as a responsible person to ensure that there were no obvious safety hazards and to co-ordinate mechanical and electrical contracts with the civil contractor. These occurred at the end of the project when the civil contractor was running down. When first employed as resident engineers the appellants maintain that it was the contractor's agent who was responsible for the site. As the works neared completion and a structure was completed, mechanical then electrical contractors came to the site and their co-ordination role was to ensure that they had access and arrived at the correct time. All these arrangements were detailed in the contract.

5. The practice at Blagdon supermarket completely overturned this situation, each of the appellants being responsible for several major projects running concurrently. This led to problems never previously encountered. Boundaries between each project and the access thereto were a constant source of problems between the major contractors, which resulted in the appellants having to utilise considerable negotiating skills to amend boundaries to enable work to proceed and to alter the contractors' proposed sequence of working to allow safe working and access.

   No provision was made for any of this in the contract documents for any of the projects and a measure of the success that we had is that we managed to complete the projects without a single major claim for disruption due to adjacent projects and had no reportable accidents.

6. With regard to the administration of the projects it was previous practice that a resident engineer was completely involved in the day to day running of the contract and dealt with the questions raised in connection with specifications, the interpretation of drawings and contract valuation. Running a number of major projects has necessitated the delegation of a lot of routine work to assistant resident engineers and quantity surveyors, with the resident engineer having to direct his attention to the management of the resources at his disposal to ensure the smooth and efficient running of the projects. He still, of course, had to have a detailed knowledge of each of the projects to enable him to settle claims, etc.

7. Three of the contracts had periods when they worked seven days a week, 24 hours each day. This required the implementation of shift systems and record keeping systems so that continuity of supervision and records was achieved. Since staff resources were limited it involved moving staff from one contract to another.

8. Previously, with regard to safety, the contractor's agent had overall responsibility for the site whereas the resident engineer had responsibility for the co-ordination of the civil contract with mechanical and electrical contracts, and operations. The resident engineer's responsibility was precisely that of any responsible person whose duty was to draw the contractor's agent's attention to any serious safety problems.

9. The situation at Blagdon supermarket was different from any other situation that the company had been involved in previously. The appellants supervised up to four major projects current at any one time. They were responsible for co-ordinating the activities of each of the contractors to ensure that individual contractor's activities did not endanger other contractors' personnel.

   The arrival of the M&E contractors not allowed for in the civil contracts led to further safety co-ordination problems.

   The situation at Blagdon supermarket has meant that the role of actively managing the safety on the site as a whole was transferred from the contractor's agent to the appellants. This is a new and additional responsibility, as far as site safety is concerned and is a fundamental aspect of the appeal.

   The appellants were responsible, as the proprietor of the site's representative, for the co-ordination of all activities on the site as a whole to ensure a safe working environment for all personnel. With the large numbers of men involved all working on overlapping sites this has proved a very demanding task, the real extent of which may only be appreciated by those with a knowledge of large construction sites.

10. The supervision of a fivefold increase in the numbers of staff has required the use of increased organisational and communication skills in order to utilise and manage them to provide an efficient contract management team. Additionally the Health and Safety Executive by its decisions to prosecute resident engineers whose staff have been involved in serious accidents on site have made it perfectly clear that it regards the resident engineers as being solely responsible for the safety of their own staff on site.

11. In conclusion the increase in duties and responsibilities involved in the running of such a large and complex scheme have been so great, that a re-grading to Grade 10 is more than justified.

Yours faithfully

Stan Izbicki
Area Official CWU

MANAGEMENT STATEMENT OF CASE

Rowland Engineering Ltd

Fosse Way
Granby
Warwickshire

To: arbitration panel   16 November

Mr W. Arnold and Mr J. Peters

The bases of the claims of both Mr Arnold and Mr Peters are increased duties and responsibilities relating to the following:

1. A wider span of control, during the past three years, when responsibility was assumed for more than one project, including responsibility for acting as engineers' representative.
2. Co-ordination of the separate contracts within each of the projects in progress.

    It is accepted that there has been a general increase in workload, and changes in contract supervision requirements since their initial appointments as resident engineers.

    Management is of the view however that the duties and responsibilities they undertake have not materially changed in character, and are accommodated within their job description. The fact that their responsibility now extends to more than one project and separate contracts within the project has not significantly altered the level at which they are required to perform.

3. They claim increased supervision arising from the responsibility for multi-projects and project values.

    There has been an additional injection of site resources to assist with work which previously they would have been expected to perform. With the exception of quantity surveying staff and clerk typists, all other subordinate staff have been taken account of in the posts' grade evaluation.

4. They further claim the additional role of 'site supervising officer' and an increased liaison role with external consultants.

    The liaison role between them and other site staff, either internal or external consultants or agents, has always been a feature of the posts, as has the responsibility for site safety. With regard to the latter it is acknowledged that the Health and Safety at Work Act has heightened safety awareness, and the higher safety profile has resulted in the formalising of their safety role as 'safety supervising officers'; nonetheless there has been no change in their responsibility for site safety.

5. In Mr Peters's case he has claimed additional duty of the development and operation of computerised systems in relation to site records and financial information.

It is recognised that he has been involved in the development of site computing facilities with other members of staff to compile site records previously kept manually. This is deemed compatible with his level of responsibility.

Having reviewed the post's grade in light of their claims of increased duties and responsibilities, management finds that there has been no change sufficient to warrant the posts' re-grading, and Grade 9 is still appropriate.

B. J. Peel
Employee Relations Officer

ASSOCIATED DOCUMENTS

Rowlands Engineering Ltd

General statement concerning the engineering function

1. The relevant engineering function in Rowlands Engineering Ltd provides a full design and construction service for all projects carried out in the West Midlands.
2. This engineering unit was restructured three years ago to enable it to cope with the increasing volume of projects contained in the capital works programme. These units comprised; three civil engineering groups, one electrical and mechanical engineering group, together with one specialist service group.
3. A copy of the revised structure for the engineering unit is enclosed.
4. Each project carried out within the engineering unit was managed from inception, throughout the whole range of activities, through to completion by a project engineer. The project engineers were responsible to a group engineer.
5. The majority of design was carried out in-house and the supervision of the construction contracts was provided by a team of permanent in-house resident engineers and clerks of works supplemented from time to time with appropriate temporary staff.
6. Each civil engineering contract was carried out under supervision of a nominated 'engineer' who was supported on site by the resident engineer and clerk of works. The nominated 'engineer' was normally a group engineer but after the restructuring could have been a principal engineer.

Rowlands Engineering Ltd

Head office

Planning department

Design and Construction Manager (JNC)
Group Engineer (11)
(Mech./Elec./Inst.)
3 Principal Assistant Engineers (9)
6 Senior Assistant Engineers (8)
8 Assistant Engineers (7)
4 Graduate Engineers (3/6)

8 Technicians
4 Group Engineers (11)
(Civils)
8 Principal Assistant Engineers (9)
16 Senior Assistant Engineers (8)
16 Assistant Engineers (7)
12 Graduate Engineers (3/6)
20 Technicians
2 Resident Engineers (9)
2 Resident Engineers (8)
4 Clerks of Works (5)
4 Clerks of Works (4)
Specialist Services Engineer (11)
Senior Assistant Engineer (8) (Specialist Design and Computing)
Senior Assistant Engineer (8) (Geotechnics)
Senior Assistant Engineer (8) (Sewerage)
Quantity Surveyor (8)
Assistant Quantity Surveyor (6)
Architectural Assistant (7)
Building Technician (4)
Chief Draughtsman (5)
7 Draughtsmen/Tracers (2)
Technical Administration Assistant (4)
1 Clerk (3)
2 Reprographics Assistants (1)
Clerk/Typist (1)
2 Clerical Assistants (1)
3 Typists (1)

Rowlands Engineering Ltd Joint Staff Council

Staff re-grading application form

Part A

General information

1. Name — W. Arnold
2. Post title — Resident Engineer
3. Grade of post — 9
4. Personal Grade (if different)
5. (a) Division or directorate — Civil Engineering
   (b) Work location — Blagdon supermarket

6. Appointment to present post   5 years
7. Date from which present
    Personal Grade applied   N/A
8. (a)   Grade claimed   10
    (b)   Effective date claimed   February
        (maximum one year retrospection,
        except for claims arising from the
        head office and dual purpose
        reorganisation, in which case two
        years maximum retrospection
        before the date of application)
9. Grounds on which the   Increased duties and
    application is made   responsibilities
10. Immediate supervisor
    (a)   Name   R. Harding
    (b)   Designation   Specialist Services Engineer
11. *For Authority Use*:
    Date form received by
    division/directorate

Increased duties and responsibilities and any other grounds

Duties and responsibilities originally attached to the post

Please state your original duties and responsibilities together with the estimated frequency of each duty, or attach a copy of the original job description for the post. Please include the number and type(s) of staff supervised.

Duties and responsibilities   **Frequency**
                          (e.g. daily, weekly,
                          monthly, etc.)

The job description originally attached to the post is attached as Appendix 1a.

At that time the staff supervised included two assistant resident engineers, one clerk of works and one typist.

Duties and responsibilities added to the post or which have changed in character or frequency, i.e. list the additional duties or increased responsibilities

Changes to job description (Appendix 1a)

Item 1
To be the engineer's representative on a number of projects at one time. Previously it was the practice for one to manage one project at one time with average values of £1–£3 m. I am at present managing a number of projects with current work valued at £8–£9 m and outstanding projects a further £5–£6 m.

Item 2
To co-ordinate projects within a multi-project scheme and co-ordinate separate contracts within those projects. In certain cases the contract boundaries have overlapped or other conflicts have arisen all of which have required increased co-ordination/negotiation duties.

Additions to job description

Item 9
To act as safety supervisor on all projects under my control including mechanical and electrical contracts. This is a major additional responsibility requiring me to monitor contractors' compliance with all regulations concerned with construction works. When, as at present, the site is occupied by more than one contractor then the level of responsibility is substantially increased with the safety supervisor having the duty of ensuring that all contractors work safely in respect of each other and NWW personnel.

Item 10
To liaise with consultants and other external agencies on site.

Item 11
To develop and operate computerised systems for site records and financial information.

I now supervise the following staff:

One assistant resident engineer – Grade 7
One assistant resident engineer – Grade 6
One assistant resident engineer – Grade 3
One assistant resident engineer – on contract
Two clerk of works – Grade 5
One clerk of works – Grade 4

One clerk of works — on contract
One quantity surveyor — Grade 8
Two quantity surveyors — consultant staff
One quantity surveyor's clerk — consultant staff
Two typists — Grade 2
Two chainboys — manual grade
see organisational chart (Appendix 2)

Instructions received from and liaison with other posts in your department

Instructions from one group engineer
Liaison with one project engineer

List any change in the nature of liaison with any instructions received from other posts in your department

Instructions from a number of group engineers
Liaison with up to four project engineers (civil)
Liaison with project engineer (mechanical/electrical)
Liaison with project co-ordinator

Internal (i.e. within the company and external contacts maintained to carry out work)

Internal contacts	Purpose
Operations	Liaison
External contacts	**Purpose**
Site agent	Supervise works

List any change in level of degree of internal and external contact

Internal contacts	Purpose
Safety advisor	Liaison
External contacts	**Purpose**
Associate of consulting QS	Staffing levels and performance
Health & safety officials	Liaison
BJAX security	Site security
Up to six site agents	Supervise works

Rowlands Engineering Ltd Joint Staff Council
Staff re-grading application form

Part A

General information

1. Name	J. Peters
2. Post title	Resident Engineer
3. Grade of Post	9
4. Personal Grade (if different)	
5. (a) Division or directorate	Civil Engineering
(b) Work location	Blagdon supermarket
6. Appointment to present post	$7\frac{1}{2}$ years
7. Date from which present	
Personal Grade applied	N/A
8. (a) Grade claimed	10
(b) Effective date claimed	February

8. (b) (maximum one year retrospection, except for claims arising from the head office and dual purpose reorganisation, in which case two years maximum retrospection before the date of application)

9. Grounds on which the application is made	Increased duties and responsibilities
10. Immediate Supervisor	
(a) Name	R. Harding
(b) Designation	Specialist Services Engineer
11. *For Authority Use*: Date form received by division/directorate	

Increased duties and responsibilities and any other grounds

Duties and responsibilities originally attached to the post

Please state your original duties and responsibilities together with the estimated frequency of each duty, or attach a copy of the original job description for the post. Please include the number and type(s) of staff supervised.

Duties and responsibilities	Frequency (e.g. daily, weekly, monthly, etc.)

The original duties and responsibilities were as the attached job description form.
The staff supervised were:
Up to two assistant resident engineers (Grade 3) ⎫
One clerk of works (Grade 6) ⎬ Daily
One typist (Grade 1) ⎭

Instructions received from and liaison with other posts in your department

Instructions from the divisional manager
Liaison with one project engineer

List any change in the nature of liaison with any instructions received from other posts in your department

Instructions from up to three group engineers
Liaison with up to four project engineers
Liaison with mechanical/electrical project engineer
Liaison with project co-ordinator
Internal (i.e. within the company and external contacts maintained to carry out work)

Internal contacts	**Purpose**
Operations	Liaison
External contacts	**Purpose**
Site agent	Supervise works

List any change in level of degree of internal and external contact

Internal contacts	**Purpose**
Safety advisor	Liaison
External contacts	**Purpose**
Associate of consulting quantity surveyors	Staffing levels and performance monitoring
BJAX security	Site security
Up to four site agents	Supervise works
Health & safety officials	Liaison

Appendix 1a

Rowlands Engineering Ltd

Job description: Resident Engineer

1. Job information
   - (a) Division: Head office
   - (b) Department: Design & Construction
   - (c) Location:
   - (d) Job Title: Resident Engineer
   - (e) Grade: 9
   - (f) Post-holder:

2. Main purposes of job:
   To control and supervise the construction of foundations, buildings and associated services carried out by contract.

3. Principal duties:
   1. to be the engineer's representative on site
   2. to ensure the works are constructed in accordance with the contract
   3. to co-ordinate separate contracts within a project
   4. to supervise staff under his control
   5. to monitor and report the contractor's progress
   6. to check the contractor's interim and final valuations of work carried out
   7. to assist the engineer in the settlement of disputes and claims
   8. to liaise with divisional operations personnel

4. Supervision exercised:
   - (a) Direct:
     Assistant resident engineer
     Other site engineers
     Clerks of works
   - (b) Indirect:

5. Supervision received:
   - (a) Direct:
     Group engineer
     or principal assistant engineer
   - (b) Indirect:
     Design and construction manager

6. Other organisational relationships
   Senior assistant engineer
   Divisional operations
   Personnel

7. Signature of post-holder

   Date:

8. Signature of section head

   Date:

Appendix 1b

The changes to the principal duties listed on the job description form are:

1. To be the engineer's representative on up to four major projects running concurrently. Approximate total value £8 m.
3. To co-ordinate on site the separate contracts within each project and to co-ordinate each of the projects with each other.
4. Supervision now includes the following staff:
   resident engineer (Grade 7)
   senior assistant resident engineer (Grade 7)
   two assistant resident engineers (Grade 5)
   two self-employed assistant resident engineers
   two clerks of works (Grade 5)
   two self-employed clerks of works
   senior quantity surveyor (Grade 8)
   senior quantity surveyor – consultant quantity surveyor
   two clerk/typists (Grade 2)

The additional duties and responsibilities are:

9. To act as site safety supervising officers on each of the projects for which we are engineer's representatives and on mechanical, electrical and instrumentation contracts for which we are not engineer's representatives.

   This is a major additional responsibility which has involved organising and chairing safety and co-ordination meetings to solve problems that occur when one contractor's activities affect another as well as ensuring that each contractor is working in a safe manner.
10. To liaise with consulting engineers and architects during the construction stage of the projects.

Appendix 2

Organisation Chart – Civil Engineering Department

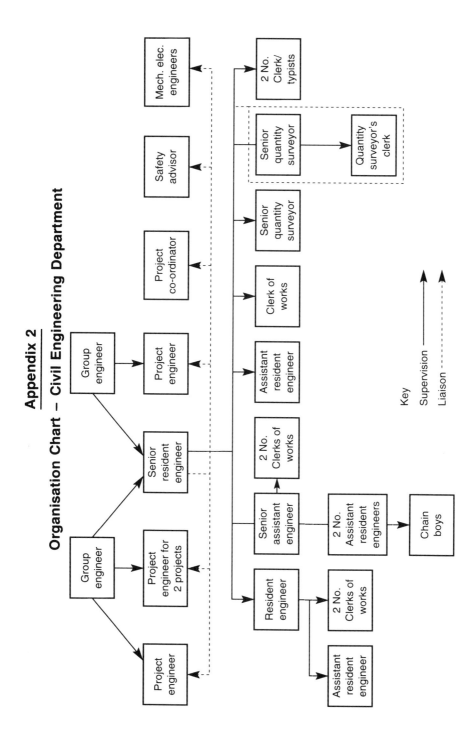

Key

Supervision ⟶

Liaison - - - - ⟶

Appendix 3
Rowlands Engineering Ltd
Head Office

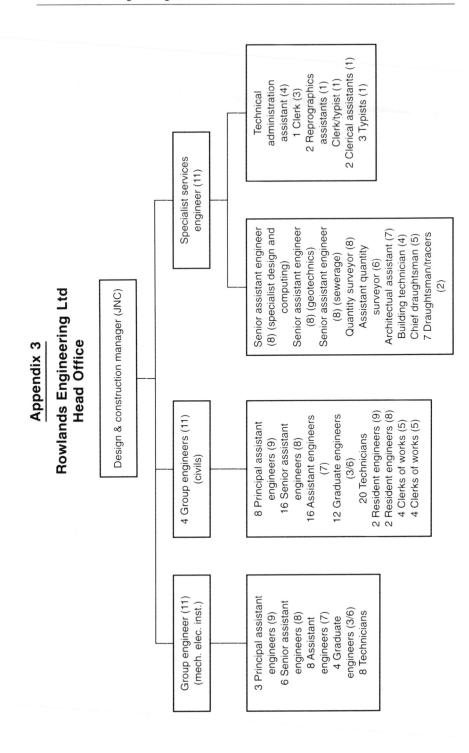

Design & construction manager (JNC)

Specialist services engineer (11)

Technical administration assistant (4)
1 Clerk (3)
2 Reprographics assistants (1)
Clerk/typist (1)
2 Clerical assistants (1)
3 Typists (1)

Senior assistant engineer (8) (specialist design and computing)
Senior assistant engineer (8) (geotechnics)
Senior assistant engineer (8) (sewerage)
Quantity surveyor (8)
Assistant quantity surveyor (6)
Architectual assistant (7)
Building technician (4)
Chief draughtsman (5)
7 Draughtsman/tracers (2)

4 Group engineers (11) (civils)

8 Principal assistant engineers (9)
16 Senior assistant engineers (8)
16 Assistant engineers (7)
12 Graduate engineers (3/6)
20 Technicians
2 Resident engineers (9)
2 Resident engineers (8)
4 Clerks of works (5)
4 Clerks of works (5)

Group engineer (11) (mech. elec. inst.)

3 Principal assistant engineers (9)
6 Senior assistant engineers (8)
8 Assistant engineers (7)
4 Graduate engineers (3/6)
8 Technicians

Rowlands Engineering Ltd Joint Staff Council Grading Appeal – Messrs W. Arnold & J. Peters

Minutes of an appeals panel held on 11 May.

Present:

Management:
Mr D. Riley – Transport
Services Manager
Mr J. Carter – Engineering
Manager
Mr B. J. Peel – Employee
Relations Officer

Union:
Mr L. Lennox – CWU Shop
Steward
Mr T. Ecclestone – CWU Shop
Steward
Ms P. Johnson – CWU Shop
Steward

Appointment of chairman

It was resolved that Mr L. Lennox be appointed Chairman

Representing the company

Mr M. Dawson – Personnel Officer

Representing the appellant

Mr S. Izbicki – Area Official CWU

Panel decision

Following consideration, the decision of the panel was given as follows: 'failure to agree'. However, the panel feels that financial recognition is appropriate in the form of a payment of an honorarium payment of £1500 per appellant. This payment would be offset if the claim was subsequently pursued and was successful.

Questions

1   How would you assess the complexity of the managerial tasks undertaken by the resident engineer?

2   Do you consider the £1500 ex gratia payment to have been a wise move on the part of the company?

3   Would a re-grading to 10 have repercussions relating to the responsibilities of other senior engineering managers?

Arbitration between

NORTHERN MINOR BANKS

and

the BUILDING SOCIETY AND BANK WORKERS UNION

(in respect of a pay claim)

Terms of reference

The terms of reference agreed by both parties were:

> 'To determine the appropriate increase in basic pay and the annual bonus for local staff to be paid from 1 April 1990.'

Documentation

The arbitrator received statements of the case from both parties prior to the hearing. He also received a comprehensive set of background documents detailing the steps toward final independent arbitration under the auspices of ACAS. Included in the documents is a copy of the agreement reached between the parties concerning the negotiation procedures which are to be adopted.

Both parties to the dispute received and studied each other's submissions.

Background to the dispute

The Northern Minor Banks group is a loose arrangement between the Lancashire Colliery Bank, the Cumbrian Woollen Bank and the Lancashire and Yorkshire Friendly Society Bank. The Lancashire Colliery Bank is the largest with 11 branches and a head office in Manchester. Arrangements between these banks extend to handling business for each other in towns where a member does not have a branch and to an informal agreement that they will pay their staff similar amounts in a similar structure.

Pay scales have tended to lag behind the major clearing banks and the union has tried to move matters forward to some form of parity. The present claim is based partly on an attempt to close this gap and partly on a comparability case. It includes a request for an increase in basic pay together with a bonus payment. There is a disagreement about the definition of bonus.

THE UNION CASE TO THE ARBITRATOR

The Building Society and Bank Workers Union

12 Cherry Street
Gorton
Manchester

18 September 1990

Dear Sir

I hereby present you with the case for the union concerning the Northern Minor Banks for the hearing to be held on 30 September 1990.

Opening remarks

It will become apparent that this is the fifth consecutive year that there has been a pay arbitration in one or other of the Northern Banks. This year the banks are acting jointly on an official basis for the first time.

Background

The associated documents show details of the claim. The procedure was followed and eventually led to conciliation at ACAS where the final position remained as an offer of 8.1 per cent across the board with no more on bonus.

As will be seen from the attached, there has been a consistent theme to the union approach. Over a period of more than 10 years we have sought to bring up the levels of pay and benefits to market level.

Part of this plan was the introduction of a bonus scheme and this was awarded by a previous arbitration. The award of last year referred to the bonus being at least partly performance related.

There was an obvious difficulty in this respect as the Cumbrian Woollen Bank is the only one of the three banks to have a proper appraisal scheme. The union side could see no realistic or viable method of operating an effective performance related scheme and stated that we would be prepared to consider any scheme put forward by the banks.

No scheme has been forthcoming and we must therefore assume that the banks have also been unable to devise a scheme. This being the case, the union feels that the only alternative is to retain an 'across the board' bonus. Our original bonus claim was for a thirteenth salary or 8.33 per cent.

At the arbitration hearing which granted the original bonus it was accepted that it would be unreasonable to expect an additional 8.33 per cent in one go. It will be seen that an initial 2.5 per cent was increased to 3.5 per cent last year but we feel that at least 5 per cent is now justified.

No doubt the banks will be stating the economic problems that they currently face. Nonetheless it is clear that this is the result of cumulative features and not a trading loss for the current year.

As far as the basic pay increase is concerned, the 'going rate' for 1990 was around 8.3 per cent and this figure was the most common.

In this respect there is little difference between the union and the banks.

Conclusion

As will be obvious from previous arbitration hearings, the bonus issue has been with us for a long time. Both the union and the banks are looking for a long term solution albeit without success so far.

In view of the difficulties outlined above we would ask the arbitrator to award an appropriate across the board increase in both basic pay and bonus.

Yours faithfully

Harold Swales
Chief Negotiator

THE EMPLOYER'S CASE TO THE ARBITRATOR

Wilkes and Howarth Solicitors

St Mary's Walk
Manchester

14 September 1990

To: the arbitrator

Dear Sir

re: Northern Minor Banks

On behalf of our clients, Lancashire Colliery Bank, Cumbrian Woollen Bank and the Lancashire and Yorkshire Friendly Society Bank please find attached the case for the employers.

We have the privilege of representing our clients at the hearing on 30 September.

Yours faithfully

Alan Boothroyd
Senior Partner

THE BANKS' CASE FOR PAY ARBITRATION

1. Scope of the arbitration

On 17 January 1990 the union wrote to the three Northern Banks, submitting identical pay claims and requesting that joint negotiations be introduced. The pay claim was for an across the board increase in basic salaries of 12 per cent, together with an increase in annual bonus to 8.33 per cent. Although the union also requested increases in large town allowances, it has been agreed that these are outside the scope of the present arbitration. A considerable time elapsed in finalising the draft procedural agreement for the joint negotiations and it was not until May that it proved possible to arrange a meeting attended by all parties to discuss matters. Further meetings were held on 28 May, 19 June and 2 July. The procedural agreement governing the negotiations was finalised at the meeting on 19 June and the banks jointly offered 8.1 per cent on salary scales from 1 April 1990 and a bonus of 3.5 per cent. The union, at the meeting on 2 July 1990 reduced their request to an 8.5 per cent increase in basic salaries and an annual bonus of 5 per cent from last year's bonus of 3.5 per cent.

Thereafter there was a conciliation meeting at ACAS on 29 July, which was unsuccessful, which has led to the present arbitration hearings.

2. Retail Prices Index

According to the Central Statistical Office the Retail Prices Index (RPI) increased by 8.1 per cent in the 12 month period from March 1989 to March 1990. The RPI provides for a base of 100 as at 13 January 1987. The figure for March 1990 was 121.4. If mortgage and housing costs are removed from these figures the underlying inflation rate falls to 6.3 per cent from March 1989 to March 1990.

3. The financial situation

The Bank of England's latest quarterly report accepted that for the time being inflationary pressures in the United Kingdom remain strong. However the report stated that the increase in the RPI was affected by special factors which were unlikely to recur. The Bank of England estimated underlying inflation was rising at only 6.5 per cent. Furthermore the report cautions against the 'further ratcheting up of wage costs' if no account was taken of the difference between headline and underlying inflation.

4. Clearing bank settlements

It is accepted by the union that employees at the Northern Banks are paid a salary equivalent to their counterparts in the clearing banks. A list of the available details of pay settlements for other banks is attached at Appendix A (*see* p. 194). From these, we submit, it is apparent that clearing bank settlements tend to be in the 8.3 per cent to 8.5 per cent pay range. However this takes no account of the particular factors affecting negotiations between the Northern Banks and the union, or the current financial difficulties facing the Northern Banks. It has been understood and accepted by the union that the benchmark figure for pay claims would be the March on March RPI figure. To an extent, as I have explained already, this is a generous measure to adopt for bank staff who are, to a large extent, free from one of the major factors in RPI, namely mortgage interest costs. A housing loan scheme with a concessional rate of interest at 5 per cent on loans up to £40 000 is available. Indeed at the meeting on 28 May 1990 the union accepted that for some while it had been the practice to use the March RPI figure.

At last year's arbitration with the Cumbrian Woollen Bank the union requested, and were given, a pay rise equivalent to the increase in the RPI from March 1988 to March 1989. While it is true that in April the increase in RPI was 9.4 per cent this should not alter the fact that the March RPI is the appropriate figure on which to base the pay settlement.

Secondly, it is again accepted by the union that the Northern Banks have been hard hit by the Bank of England's matrix regarding provisions for doubtful debts. It is clear that the Northern Banks are coming under pressure to curb costs, in order to justify their continued level of operations within niche markets.

Both these factors we submit should be taken into account in confirming the banks' across the board pay offer of 8.1 per cent as an appropriate one in the circumstances. We would additionally point out that there is a certain amount of wage drift, given that there are annual increments also paid in addition to the percentage rises agreed upon.

5.1 Bonus: The basis for a bonus

As the arbitrators will be aware the Northern Banks have not been obliged to make payment of a bonus to staff until very recently. The issue was first referred to arbitration with Lancashire Colliery Bank in 1987 when the union demanded a bonus payment of 8.33 per cent, i.e. a thirteenth month of salary. The arbitrators, however, simply stated that some form of bonus payment should be introduced as part of 1988 pay settlements. No bonus was awarded at this stage and no details were laid down, on the understanding that the actual bonus payment would be negotiated between the bank and the union.

The union, however, contended that they had been awarded a final bonus payment of 8.33 per cent to be reached over a period of time and accordingly accepted bonus payments of 2.5 per cent in 1988.

In 1989 again the parties could not negotiate successfully and the issue was taken to arbitration with the Cumbrian Woollen Bank when the arbitrator awarded a bonus of 3.5 per cent.

During the current negotiations again the union maintains that the banks have to raise their bonus payments to the level of a month's salary by graduated increase in bonus payments every year. The banks are unable to understand this demand for bonus by way of additional wages and consider that it is absolutely vital to clarify the nature of this payment before the amount of payment is deliberated.

Looked at in principle, the Northern Banks could be obliged to make a payment of a bonus in one of three ways.

Firstly, the obligations to pay bonus could be by virtue of the employees' contracts. This is clearly not the case.

Secondly, the banks could be obliged to make additional payments as a *discretionary bonus* in which case the union's claim for eventual 8.33 per cent or the claim of 5 per cent for the current year is very much in excess of the schemes operating in other banks in the UK. Even the present offer of 3.5 per cent made by the banks would be considered generous in this context.

Thirdly, a bonus would be payable in the form of a *profit sharing* arrangement, preferably linked up with a performance related bonus scheme as was awarded in the last year's arbitration. In their present financial circumstances, the banks would argue that they should not be burdened with any bonus payment, given their financial results and the total lack of profits to share by way of bonus payment.

We will deal further with why the principle of the union's claim for 'bonus' is unsound, but we request that the arbitrator, as a matter of importance, should outline to the parties the basis on which any bonus payment is awarded. This will reduce the scope for complication in future negotiations between the parties, since all parties will know that a bonus is payable on the basis of, say, custom and practice.

5.2 Bonus denotes merit, not across the board pay rise

In last year's arbitration with the Cumbrian Woollen Bank the arbitrator recommended that 'in view of the uncertainties regarding the bonus scheme I recommend that the parties discuss and negotiate a revised scheme which should be performance related to at least some degree'.

This principle that a bonus was merit related was accepted by the union at a meeting on 28 May 1990 but brushed aside with the assertion that the union did not consider the bank capable of assessing individual performance. This is dealt with further below, but with respect to the union this of course begged the question as to whether a bonus was to be assessed in relation to individual performance or the bank's performance.

The union has demanded a flat rate 5 per cent pay rise to all staff on the basis that no negotiations on the framework for a bonus have taken place. The arbitrator will note that the 1989 arbitration award did not decide that the Cumbrian Woollen Bank should initiate discussions in relation to profit or performance related pay, and it is therefore disingenuous of the union to state that because no deliberations had taken place, it is able therefore to seek a flat rate across the board salary rise for all staff. If the union is pushing for a bonus scheme to be introduced then nothing prevents them suggesting such a scheme.

There are three arguments as to why the union's request for an across the board pay rise is in principle one which should be rejected by the arbitrator.

Firstly, the arbitration last year for the Cumbrian Woollen Bank specifically stated that the bonus scheme to be negotiated by the parties should be performance related to at least some degree. Secondly, the very concept of a bonus, we would submit, denotes a reward for meritorious services. The word 'bonus' is of course derived from the Latin for good. Finally, it is significant that many other major banks do not have an across the board bonus of this nature. Details obtained from IRS indicate that Lloyds, Barclays, National Westminster and the Royal Bank of Scotland either have a profit share or no bonus at all. In practical terms what the union seeks today is a pay rise of 13.5 per cent. This is as part of an avowed policy to obtain a flat rate bonus of 8.33 per cent for all members of staff. This cannot be correct.

It is true that the Northern Banks, in an effort to maintain goodwill and avoid the arbitration which has since become necessary, have offered a 3.5 per cent flat rate bonus. As an expression of goodwill this should not be construed as an acceptance of a principle that a bonus should be paid to members of staff without regard to merit, without regard to effort and without regard to the financial success of the banks. It was for this reason that the banks tried to clarify before the hearing the scope of the arbitration with regard to bonus. To date the union has flatly refused to accept that a bonus should be a reward, and has looked on it as an entitlement for all members of staff. We submit to the arbitrators that this is clearly incorrect.

6.1 If flat rate bonus awarded

It is questionable whether any bonus should be paid to the staff even if the arbitrator is minded to accept the union's claim that any bonus paid should be a flat rate bonus. Clearly the bonus cannot be considered without careful consideration of the banks' present financial state.

There has been an adverse change in the financial position with regards to profitability of all the Northern Banks resulting in sizeable losses, and it has become a serious situation for all Northern Banks to reduce their overheads – particularly since they have limited opportunity as compared to other clearing banks who are also showing poor results due to provisioning for bad debts.

The result has been the necessity for support from the respective head offices by way of remittances. The remittances made from the reserves of the three Northern Banks in the current year to meet losses aggregate £2.4 m.

The Bank of England has also emphasised to the Northern Banks that they must provide sufficient funds to cover the bad debts within the next two years. In the circumstances, the banks are endeavouring to reduce their operational costs and limit their losses for their very survival.

However, the banks would not go back on the bonus offered and therefore we submit that the arbitrator should award only a 3.5 per cent bonus as offered as a goodwill gesture by the banks.

As salary and annual bonus is one of the various measures to control operational costs, staff should share the banks' concern and make their contribution by accepting the reasonable offer in the present adverse financial situation.

6.2   If the bonus award is based on custom and practice

The arbitrator may decide that in principle a bonus for staff should be based on custom and practice at other banks. Details of flat rate bonuses paid to staff by other banks are sketchy, but so far as we are aware Midland Bank pays a bonus in November of 2.5 per cent, and Abbey National paid a £200 bonus to its staff. Lloyds and Standard Chartered paid discretionary bonuses worth 2.5 per cent last year. Therefore the Northern Banks submit that the level of bonus offered this year is more than generous, in the light of industry practice.

7.0   If the arbitrators award a merit bonus

We submit that the best course would be to recommend that the parties enter into negotiations immediately over a merit related bonus. The arbitrators may feel that a recommendation should be added that any resultant bonus will be up to a maximum of 3.5 per cent of salary. The Northern Banks would be prepared to consider enlisting the assistance of ACAS to draw up a suitable scheme. It is, however, clear to avoid future difficulties that the arbitrator should rule on the nature of the appropriate bonus for employees, to enable parties to avoid the difficulties which have arisen in relation to the scheme.

We would therefore go further and ask the arbitrator to recommend that negotiations be directed towards the introduction of a profit share scheme. The union has expressed concern over the introduction of procedures for assessments of employees at the Northern Banks, and clearly it would be a weighty administrative task given that the banks do not at present have adequate assessment schemes in place. A profit scheme would be much easier to operate, and would have the logical advantage that a bonus would only be paid to staff when the employing bank's performance merited it.

Appendix A

Details of pay awards

Date	Bank	%
1 January 1990	National Westminster	8.3
1 February 1990	Barclays Bank	8.4
		+ 0.75
1 April 1990	Royal Bank of Scotland	8.3
1 April 1990	Yorkshire Bank	8.3
1 April 1990	Lloyds Bank	8.3
1 April 1990	Standard Chartered	8.3 or £500
1 April 1990	Bank of Scotland	9.4 (over 13.5 months)
21 April 1990	TSB	8.3 or £520
1 June 1990	Midland	8.3 + £75–£125

ASSOCIATED DOCUMENTS

1. 17 January 1990   Pay claim letter from BSBWU to Cumbrian Woollen Bank

2. 5 May 1990   Minutes of meeting between BSBWU and representatives of the three banks

3. 28 May 1990   Minutes of meeting between BSBWU and representatives of the three banks

4. 19 June 1990   Minutes of meeting between BSBWU and representatives of the three banks. The negotiating and procedure agreement finally agreed follows

5. 2 July 1990   Minutes of meeting between BSBWU and representatives of the three banks

6. 20 July 1990   Letter to ACAS from Lancashire Colliery Bank

7. 24 July 1990   Letter to Lancashire Colliery Bank from ACAS

8. 29 July 1990   Reference to arbitration document

9. 13 August 1990   Letter to BSBWU from Wilkes and Howarth Solicitors

10. 27 August 1990   Letter to BSBWU from Wilkes and Howarth Solicitors

11. 27 August 1990   Letter to Wilkes and Howarth Solicitors from BSBWU

12. 1 September 1990   Letter to BSBWU from Wilkes and Howarth Solicitors

13. 2 September 1990   Letter to Cumbrian Woollen Bank from BSBWU

14. 5 September 1990   Letter to BSBWU from Wilkes and Howarth

15. 9 September 1990   Letter to Cumbrian Woollen Bank from BSBWU

16. 16 September 1990   Letter to the arbitrator from Wilkes and Howarth Solicitors

Building Society and Bank Workers Union

12 Cherry Street
Gorton
Manchester

Our ref: HS/SJH

17 January 1990

Mr R. Pollard
General Manager
Cumbrian Woollen Bank
Castle Square
Carlisle

Dear Mr Pollard

Pay Claim 1990

On behalf of the BSBWU members in the Cumbrian Woollen Bank, I set out below our pay claim to be effective from 1 April 1990.

1. An across the board increase in basic salaries of 12 per cent.
2. Large town allowance to be increased to £750.
3. The annual bonus to be increased to 8.33 per cent.

I look forward to hearing from you in due course.

Yours sincerely

Harold Swales
Chief Negotiating Officer

Meeting between representatives of the three banks and BSBWU held on 5 May 1990

Present:

Mr S. Ryton – Lancashire Colliery Bank
Mr C. Bolton – Cumbrian Woollen Bank
Mr W. Burton – Lancs. & Yorks. Friendly Society Bank

Mr H. Swales – BSBWU
Mr A. King – LCB Chapel
Mrs H. Tomkins – CWB Chapel
Mr W. Haslett – LYFSB Chapel

Mr Ryton said that the three banks had decided that he should chair the meetings and that the purpose of this meeting was to agree the proposed procedural agreement (which had been sent to the union on 4 April 1990) before the union substantiated its pay claim.

Mr Swales acknowledged that this was the position and said that the union had a number of points it wished to raise on the procedural agreement, the details of which had already been advised to Mr Burton. Mr Swales said that the union was concerned about the quorum and the time period set out in the procedure which should, in the union's view, be shortened – otherwise in the event of a dispute there could be long time scales involved.

Following a short discussion, the following amendments to the procedure were agreed:

Paragraph 3

Insert in the penultimate line after 'obligations, although the' 'banks and the'.

Paragraph 7 (ii)

Insert in the penultimate line after 'and the banks' 'and the union'.

Paragraph 7 (iii)

Delete and insert 'The membership of the JNC will not normally be less than six and the representatives from each side will not normally be less than three'.

Paragraph 9 (ii)

Delete '30 (thirty)' in the second line and fifth line and replace with '15 (fifteen)' in each case. After 'working days' in antipenultimate line insert 'or such other period as agreed between the parties...'.

Mr Swales added, however, that the main point was that the union wished to retain a compulsory arbitration clause which already existed in the agreements between the union and the Northern Banks. Mr Burton expressed surprise and concern that this major issue should have been raised at this late stage, particularly as he understood that the draft agreement (which had been accepted in principle by the union in 1986) contained voluntary arbitration and that the union had recently agreed with the Lancashire and Yorkshire Friendly Society Bank that a revised procedure should contain a voluntary arbitration clause. He added that all the clearing banks had voluntary arbitration and that the union had agreed to this. Mr Swales said that in the case of the clearing banks, the union had no alternative other than to accept voluntary arbitration and compulsory arbitration was still common in the smaller provincial banks with whom the union had agreements. Mr Burton said that the latter point may be so in agreements that were signed many years ago but asked Mr Swales to give details of any relatively new agreement.

Mr Swales quoted a Scottish Bank.

Mr Burton also said that compulsory arbitration was unpopular with employers and many unions because experience showed that it tended to influence negotiations when at the back of everyone's mind was the thought that the issue could always be decided by an independent arbitrator. This in Mr Burton's view sometimes took away the motivation to obtain a settlement. Employers generally – particularly in industries like banking which are labour intensive – were more and more concerned about automatically allowing decisions having a direct effect on costs to a third party who have no responsibility for ensuring that the business is successful. Mr Ryton stressed that the banks were not refusing arbitration, only suggesting a change from compulsory to voluntary. Mr Haslett insisted that the union wished to have the right to refer a matter to arbitration as he believed this could speed up the process of settling a claim. Mr Burton retorted that that was the point which concerned him insofar as with compulsory arbitration there was a tendency not to have serious negotiations but to hand over the responsibility to someone else who, by definition, is always likely to make an award somewhere between the employer's last offer and the union's claim.

Mr Swales said that it would not be the union's intention to refer the matter to arbitration without due consideration as there was a considerable amount of work involved.

Mr Bolton said, nevertheless, in every year since 1987 the union had invoked the arbitration clause against one or other of the banks.

Mr Ryton said that the banks' representatives at the meeting had no mandate to change this particular clause and therefore the matter would have to be discussed by the general managers of the three banks. He was very concerned about the ensuing delay in commencing negotiations on the pay claim. He advised the union that the banks would make their response at the meeting on 28 May.

Mr Burton added that meanwhile the union should consider how serious it believed this issue to be and if it was not possible to reach agreement on this particular issue then it would not be possible for the three banks to negotiate collectively with the union. Mr Swales said he recognised the position.

The meeting closed.

Meeting between representatives of the three banks and BSBWU held on 28 May 1990

Present:

Mr S. Ryton – Lancashire Colliery Bank
Mr C. Bolton – Cumbria Woollen Bank
Mr W. Burton – Lancs. & Yorks. Friendly Society Bank

Mr H. Swales – BSBWU
Mr A. King – LCB Chapel
Mrs H. Tomkins – CWB Chapel
Mr W. Haslett – LYFSB Chapel

The minutes of the meeting held on 5 May were agreed.

Mr Burton said that the three banks had considered carefully the union's view that there should be 'compulsory arbitration' in the proposed procedure agreement but the banks were still of the view that they wished to have 'voluntary arbitration'. Mr Burton said that the banks' case had been made clear at the previous meeting.

Mr Swales replied that the union was determined to have 'compulsory arbitration' and if it could not be achieved then the union was prepared to revert to the existing system whereby it negotiated with the three banks separately and he had a mandate in that event to register 'first failure to agree' with the banks in respect of the pay claim which had been lodged in January. Mr Swales did not consider there was any 'half-way house' on this issue and said that the union's position arose from the concern of members to what appeared to them to be the banks' continuing delaying tactics. The settlement date of 1 April had long passed and arguments were still taking place over the procedure agreement.

Mr Burton acknowledged that there had been a delay but it had taken time to produce a procedure agreement and he had been under the impression that it would gain acceptance from the union, as it was based on an agreement which the union had had previously with the Association of Independent Banks, albeit the agreement had not actually been signed – and that it was only on the day of the last meeting (5 May) that the major issue had been raised by the union. The banks asked for a recess to consider the matter.

Following the recess, Mr Burton said that, in order to break the apparent impass, the banks, while still wishing to have 'voluntary arbitration' in the procedure, would be prepared to give an undertaking that for 1990 only if it was not possible to reach agreement and the union invoked the arbitration clause, the banks would not refuse arbitration. The banks would be prepared to give this undertaking in writing, if necessary.

After a short discussion, Mr Swales said that this compromise was acceptable to the union and therefore they would be prepared to sign the procedure agreement as drafted.

It was agreed that Mr Burton would circulate the procedure agreement with the revised paragraphs that were agreed at the last meeting for it to be signed by the union and the banks at the next meeting.

Mr Burton asked the union to substantiate its claims and Mr Swales replied as follows.

Pay

Mr Swales said for some while it had been the practice between the union and the banks to use the 31 March RPI figure (published in April) as the guideline RPI figure in respect of claims and in March 1990 the RPI was 8.1 per cent. He continued that there had been settlements in the clearing banks in excess of this figure and said that even if the banks paid an increase in line with the RPI that would only maintain the status quo as far the union members were concerned and would not give them any 'new money'. Mr Burton disputed this and said that there were elements of the RPI figures that did not apply to all staff, for example, a substantial number of staff had house loans with the banks and therefore were not subject to the substantial increase in mortgage rates which is reflected in the RPI figure. Mr Swales acknowledged this but said that there were an equally large number of staff who had second mortgages – particularly as generally speaking they were only able to borrow from the banks up to a maximum of approximately £40 000. Mr Swales also said that since March the RPI was continuing to rise. Mr Burton said it was not acceptable for the union to refer to the RPI applicable after the settlement date. He was sure that the union would not accept any arguments from the banks if the RPI were falling.

Annual bonus

Mr Swales said that the claim for 8.33 per cent was a figure (i.e. one thirteenth salary) which had been set by the union some while ago which originally the union had established as being round about the figure that corresponded to that which the clearing banks paid in respect of annual bonus and profit sharing. It was this figure which the union had used during the arbitration hearing between the union and the Lancashire and Yorkshire Bank in respect of 1988. Mr Swales acknowledged that in the Cumbrian Woollen Bank's arbitration award in respect of 1989, the arbitrator had said that the annual bonus should be negotiated between the bank and the union and in the arbitrator's view should be 'performance related'.

The union also accepted that it would be unrealistic to expect the banks to concede an annual bonus of 8.33 per cent this year but believed that the banks should be willing to progress towards this figure.

In response to questions from Mr Burton, the union confirmed that although it accepted the principle of a bonus being related to the individual's performance it did not believe that the banks had the machinery or systems to be able to do this and the union was looking for a settlement which would ensure that members in all three banks received a similar percentage of their basic pay as the bonus.

The union also stated that it did not believe that any 'performance related' element should apply to the existing annual bonus of 3.5 per cent.

Large town allowance

Mr Swales said he was willing to defer discussion on this matter while present negotiations continued although the union believed that there were special circumstances regarding the areas where the Northern Banks paid large town allowance and therefore in the union's view there should be a substantial increase in the allowance irrespective of what may or may not happen in the clearing banks.

The banks agreed to respond to the union's claim at a meeting arranged for 19 June 1990.

Meeting between representatives of the three banks and the BSBWU held on 19 June 1990

Present:

Mr S. Ryton – Lancashire Colliery Bank
Mr C. Bolton – Cumbrian Woollen Bank
Mr W. Burton – Lancs. & Yorks. Friendly Society Bank

Mr H. Swales – BSBWU
Mr A. King – LCB Chapel
Mrs H. Tomkins – CWB Chapel
Mr W. Haslett – LYFSB Chapel

The minutes of the meeting held on 28 May were agreed.

Mr Swales, however, requested certain clarification about the reference on 'voluntary arbitration' mentioned in the last meeting's minutes. He explained that there is a feeling among his members that the banks' undertaking agreeing not to refuse arbitration will be for the year 1990 only.

It was clarified by Mr Burton that the present agreement is for 1990 and the union has a right to terminate this agreement with due notice. It was agreed to note that:

'Union has acknowledged that this was the position and wishes to reserve the right to seek an amendment in respect of arbitration if it is not possible to reach agreement.'

After this discussion, the procedural agreement was agreed and signed by the union's and banks' representatives. The copies were distributed to each of the representatives for their record.

Pay

Mr Burton explained that there is a dramatic change in the financial position as regards the profitability of all minor banks in the UK. He also explained that there are huge losses and it has become a serious situation for all minor banks, particularly since they have limited opportunity as compared to other clearing banks, who are also showing losses due to provisions made for bad debts. The Bank of England has also emphasised to all minor banks the need to provide sufficiently for the bad debts within a period of three years. In the circumstances banks are endeavouring to curtail the operational costs and increase the profitability to the greatest extent possible. Banks feel that staff members should share the banks' concern and make their contribution by accepting the reasonable pay increase offered as follows:

1. *Across the board increase*: 8.1 per cent on salaries and salary scales from 1 April 1990. This proposal is to match with the RPI figure of 31 March 1990.
2. *Annual bonus*: no increase in the current annual bonus rate of 3.5 per cent.
3. *Large town allowance*: it was agreed that discussion on these items would be deferred.

The union rejected the banks' proposal on items 1. and 2. and registered 'first failure to agree' under the terms of the procedural agreement.

While rejecting the banks' proposal on items 1. and 2., Mr Swales said that they accept the present serious problems of the minor banks and are also aware of Bank of England's requirements. As regards the annual bonus, Mr Swales said that in other minor banks, even though they are making losses, they are still paying a bonus.

Mr Ryton and other representatives of the banks explained to the union that the annual bonus at present is paid, in effect, as an additional wage being entirely a non-performance bonus even though there has been no substantial performance change by banks in recent years.

The total remuneration package has thus been increasing as follows:

Year	Pay increase + (%)	Annual bonus (%)	Total remuneration (%)
1987	7.0	–	7.0
1988	7.0	2.5	9.5
1989	7.9	3.5	11.4
1990 (proposed)	8.1	3.5	11.6

It was also explained to the union that recently Midland Bank and Barclays Bank have opted for reduction of staff as their cost control measure.

The minor banks feel that salary and annual bonus are one of the various measures to control operational costs, staff members ought to consider the offer made by Northern Banks favourably.

Mr Swales, however, maintained that in terms of the mandate given to him by the membership he would reject the offer and register 'first failure to agree' under the terms of the procedural agreement. Mr Burton asked Mr Swales to substantiate the reasons for registering 'first failure to agree' to which Mr Swales did not respond.

Mr Ryton urged upon the union officials to communicate with their membership to seek reasonable mandate in view of the difficult business scenario. All the banks offered full co-operation to the union representatives in this regard with a view to settling the issue amicably and swiftly.

In view of the 'first failure to agree' it was decided to hold a further meeting at 2.30 p.m. on 2 July 1990.

Negotiating and procedure agreement

1. Parties

This is an agreement between Lancashire Colliery Bank, Cumbrian Woollen Bank and the Lancashire and Yorkshire Friendly Society Bank, hereinafter referred to as 'the banks' and the Building Society and Bank Workers Union, hereinafter referred to as 'the union'.

2. The intention of the agreement

It is intended by this agreement to provide a negotiating machinery for the banks to negotiate with the union and their employees to be represented by the union. The banks therefore recognise the sole right of the union to represent and negotiate in respect of the employees in the banks.

3. Scope of the agreement

The union, for its part, accepts that its area of representation is for staff employed by the banks. The agreement applies only to the terms and conditions of employment as set out in Appendix 1, together with such other terms and conditions as may be agreed in future by the parties; for the avoidance of doubt, it should be noted that formal agreement or disagreement between the parties to this agreement arising out of this agreement may be reached only on matters covered by Appendix 1. It is also agreed that while this agreement is in force matters covered by Appendix 1 will be excluded from the scope of recognition and procedure agreements between the union and individual banks and the agreements are amended to this extent. This agreement is solemnly binding in honour, but it is not intended to give rise to any legal obligations, although the banks and the union will take all practical steps to ensure and maintain the observance of this agreement.

4. Definitions

Definitions used in this agreement are:

(a) 'Joint Negotiating Council' (JNC) – the meeting of the banks and the union representatives according to the rules and procedures set out in this agreement.

(b) 'Participant' – any party to the JNC.

5. General principles

(a) The banks and the union have a common objective in the long term in ensuring the efficiency and prosperity of the negotiating banks and the benefit of their employees and customers.

(b) The banks recognise the union's responsibility to represent the legitimate and reasonable interests of its members and to work for improved conditions of employment for its members within the framework and scope of this agreement.

(c) The banks agree to refrain from lock-out and the union agrees to refrain from instigating industrial action until all the procedures for resolving issues set out in this agreement have been exhausted; the union further agrees to take all reasonable steps to prevent industrial action until such procedures are exhausted as aforesaid.

(d) The banks agree that before any of the banks implement any alterations to terms and conditions of employment covered by the terms of this agreement, it will inform the union of the proposed change. Thereafter the parties will seek to resolve any consequent issue through the negotiating procedures set out in this agreement.

6. Meetings

(a) Meetings between representatives of the banks and the union will normally be held during working hours and on the premises of one of the banks. As a rule, unless otherwise agreed, the union official and/or representative and the banks, as the case may be, shall request such a meeting at least 15 (fifteen) working days in advance, indicating the items to be discussed.

(b) Where an urgent issue covered by this agreement is to be resolved which requires immediate discussion between the banks and union, a request to the banks for a meeting in working hours will be considered against the need to maintain the operation of the banks and allowed where appropriate in the light of this consideration provided that the banks will use their best endeavours to come to such urgent meetings as required.

7. Operation of the JNC

(a) There shall be a combined joint negotiating council called the Joint Negotiation Council (JNC).

(b) The union shall be entitled to be represented on the JNC by one participant from each bank (or such lesser number as the union may decide) and the participants will be full time employees of each bank referred to above. In addition the union shall be entitled to be represented by one full time official. The banks shall be represented by the office bearers and by one participant from each bank, or such lesser number as decided by the banks. One of the banks' participants shall act as chairman and the banks and the union also have the right to have present at the JNC special guests from time to time.

(c)   The membership of the JNC will not normally be less than six and the representatives from each side will not normally be less than three.

(d)   The banks will appoint a secretary for all meetings of the JNC and be responsible for the circulation of agendas and the production of minutes.

(e)   A regular programme of not more than four meetings shall be agreed between the parties towards the end of each calendar year for the whole of the following year.

(f)   Additional meetings as may be necessary may be called at the request of either party at a time and place convenient to both parties.

(g)   Either the union or the banks may submit proposals for any JNC, but these must be submitted to the secretary of the JNC seven working days before a meeting or, if both parties agree, be dealt with under any other business.

(h)   Formal agreement or disagreement may be reached only on matters covered by Appendix 1.

(i)   There are no voting arrangements. Where a proposal cannot be agreed upon, and so declared by both parties at a meeting, then the procedure set out in the section covering collective disputes and consultative procedures may apply.

8.   Negotiating collective disputes and consultative procedures

(a)   The banks and the union agree to carry out the procedures set out in this agreement and that it is in their mutual interest to ensure that all issues arising between them shall be considered and resolved at the earliest stage possible and as speedily as possible.

(b)   The procedures for collective disputes and claims together with the arrangements for conciliation and arbitration are set out in Appendix 2 of this agreement.

9.   Further consideration of differences

(a)   If at a JNC meeting the two parties are unable to reach agreement upon a proposal or a modification of a proposal which comes within the scope of Appendix 1, then either party may register a 'first failure to agree'.

(b)   Once a 'first failure to agree' has been registered a further meeting must be called and held within 15 (fifteen) working days to reconsider the proposal. Subsequent meetings on the same subject may be called at intervals of not more than 15 (fifteen) working days or such other period as agreed between the parties until either agreement has been reached or a 'second failure to agree' has been registered by either party.

(c)   Once a 'second failure to agree' has been registered, either party may, within 15 (fifteen) working days, apply to the Advisory, Conciliation and Arbitration Service (ACAS) for conciliation and the other party will use its best endeavours to assist ACAS.

(d)   After a 'second failure to agree' has been registered, then either party may, within 25 (twenty-five) working days or within 10 (ten) working days of the end of the conciliation as defined by ACAS, whichever is the later, request arbitration and the other party must respond within 10 (ten) working days notifying either agreement to arbitration, or rejection of arbitration. In the event of agreement to arbitration the procedure as described in Appendix 2 shall be effected.

10. Alteration and terminations

(a)   This agreement may be altered without limit by mutual agreement between the banks and the union. Either party wishing to amend or modify the agreement shall give 3 (three) months' written notice to the other party of its proposals, and the notice shall contain full details of the proposed amendments.

(b)   This agreement may be terminated by either party giving 6 (six) months', or such other period agreed between the parties, written notice to the other of its intention.

Signed on behalf of: *Signed on behalf of the union*:
Cumbrian Woollen Bank

(C. Bolton)   (H. Swales)
Lancashire Colliery Bank   Chief Negotiating Officer
                                  Building Society and Bank
                                  Workers Union

(S. Ryton)   (A. King)
Lancashire & Yorkshire Friendly   LCB Chapel
Society Bank

(W. Burton)   (Mrs H. Tomkins)
                                  CWB Chapel

                                  (W. Haslett)
                                  LYFSB Chapel

Date (19 June 1990)

Appendix 1

Terms and conditions of employment covered by this agreement

1. Annual basic salary negotiations
2. Large town allowance
3. Annual bonus

Appendix 2

Arbitration procedure

Any difference or dispute which, in accordance with the agreement is to be referred to arbitration, shall be referred to an arbitrator who shall be from a list provided by ACAS by agreement between the parties to this agreement. If, within 14 (fourteen) days of the receipt of the written notice of agreement to arbitration, the parties to this agreement fail to agree upon an arbitrator then a person shall be nominated by ACAS on the application of either of the parties of this agreement to ACAS.

The following provisions shall apply to any reference to arbitration under the above clause namely:

1. Each of the parties to the reference shall proceed without delay to implement the reference and use its best endeavours to secure that the arbitration shall be constituted and the reference heard without any avoidable delay and in any case within 6 (six) weeks of the date of the reference of the dispute or difference to arbitration.
2. The banks shall be required to divulge information which is deemed consistent with good industrial relations practice, having regard to the relevant codes of practice.
3. Neither of the parties to the reference shall be represented before the arbitrator by counsel or solicitors unless at least 7 (seven) days before the hearing it shall have notified the other party to the reference of its intention to be so represented.
4. The reference shall be heard and determined by the arbitrator in private unless the parties to the reference shall otherwise agree.
5. The arbitrator shall have no power to make an award or order for the payment of costs by either of the parties to the reference to the other, but any fees or expenses payable to the arbitrator shall, unless otherwise agreed between the parties to the reference, be borne by them in equal shares.
6. Where in an endeavour to settle the dispute the parties hereto reach an agreement with regard to the dispute in question before the arbitrator's award, such agreement shall be produced in writing and signed by the arbitrator and copies given to each party. Such formalised agreement shall take effect from the date of signing or from such other date as the arbitrator may decide and the award made in respect of the reference shall take such agreement into account.
7. The banks and the union undertake to be bound by the award made by a duly constituted arbitrator following a valid reference in accordance with Appendix 2.

Meeting between representatives of the three banks and BSBWU held on 2 July 1990

Present

Mr R. Wilkinson – Lancashire Colliery Bank
Mr C. Bolton – Cumbrian Woollen Bank
Mr C. Williams – Lancs. & Yorks. Friendly Society Bank
Mr H. Swales – BSBWU
Mr A. King ⎫
Mrs H. Tomkins ⎬ Bank Chapels of BSBWU
Mr W. Haslett ⎭

The minutes of the meeting held on 19 June 1990 were agreed, subject to the following:

Mr Swales said that:

1. some of the points agreed by BSBWU were not elaborated in the minutes and suggested that a steno should be provided for noting down the minutes of the meeting to eliminate the above omissions and;
2. the correction as regard to annual bonus, i.e. annual bonus for 1989 and 1990 should be shown as 1 per cent and 0 per cent instead of 3.5 per cent each, respectively.

Mr Wilkinson and other members of the banks agreed to Mr Swales's suggestion to provide a steno apart from present quorum of representatives and also decided that the steno will be provided by the bank when the meeting will be arranged in future.

Mr Bolton explained that the percentage shown under column 'annual bonus' is a percentage of bonus paid/to be paid by the bank and not percentage increase over last year and hence the figures of percentage are correct.

Mr Wilkinson asked the union about mandate from their members on the point of pay claims and annual bonus.

Mr Swales said that they have not held a separate meeting of their members or their representatives nor have they visited the branches in the respective banks but by personal contacts at the main office and over the telephone with branches, the representatives have consulted their members and all are supporting the union's registering 'first failure to agree' and therefore, their earlier claim still stands, i.e. 1. across the board increase in basic salaries of 12 per cent and 2. the annual bonus to be increased to 8.33 per cent.

Mr Williams asked whether the union has enlightened its members of the present situation of the minor banks. Mr Swales explained that in view of obvious reasons as agreed with the banks, they have not disclosed the same to its members. While agreeing with the Bank of England's guidelines for providing for bad debts, he stressed that at present inflation has increased as compared to the March 1990 figure of 8.1 per cent and hence while deciding the pay increase the present inflation rate should also be considered.

Mr Bolton pointed out that last year, in the Cumbrian Woollen Bank award, 7.9 per cent pay rise was awarded on the basis of the inflation rate in March, 1989 and it was also what the union had desired. Secondly, if the union is saying that if they want present inflation rate as against March 1990 rate, then if the inflation is reduced below the March level, whether it will be acceptable to them. Mr Swales did not accept this. Further he explained that they are not revising their earlier proposal and it is the banks' responsibility to advise their staff of the banks' serious problems.

Mr King said that they have indirectly contacted the members and explained about the bank's present problems.

Mr Bolton stressed the point that in the last meeting it was decided that the union will arrange a meeting of members during office hours at the main office and in personal visits to branches to take a fresh mandate for pay in 1990 and, since it has not been arranged, the banks are still agreeable to provide the facility for such a meeting. The union, if it wishes, can have more time to obtain a fresh mandate.

Mr Swales did not agree to the suggestion. Mr Haslett said that they have 99 per cent support for the representatives' decisions on the pay claim and registering 'first failure to agree'.

Mr Swales further advised that their claim for annual bonus is not 8.33 per cent but a stagewise increase in a phased manner and this is the fourth and final year as per the Lancashire & Yorkshire bank award.

Mr Bolton once again explained that the Northern Minor Banks' profitability does not justify any payment of bonus but in view of the earlier offer of 3.5 per cent annual bonus, the banks are not denying the annual bonus by going back for nil bonus.

Mr Williams also suggested to the union to reconsider their proposal in the light of losses/considerably lower profitability suffered by the banks.

On this, Mr Swales quantified their proposal as follows:

1. Across the board increase in basic salaries of 8.5 per cent.
2. Annual bonus to be increased to 5 per cent from last year's bonus of 3.5 per cent.

Mr Wilkinson suggested a short recess and asked the union to reconsider its proposal.

After the recess, Mr Swales said that there was no change in the revised claim. Mr Bolton insisted the union take 15 working days more for reconsidering the revised claim in line with the banks' offer.

However, Mr Swales, denying the suggestion, continued his stand, saying that the feedback from members is quite clear and further time will be a waste of time.

Looking to the union's stand, Mr Wilkinson registered a 'second failure to agree'.

Accepting this, Mr Swales suggested that since the banks have registered a 'second failure to agree', the banks should apply to the Advisory, Conciliation and Arbitration Service as being the next step according to the negotiating and procedure agreement.

This suggestion was accepted by the banks.

Lancashire Colliery Bank

Head Office
College Street
Bolton

Private and Confidential

Mr Riley
Conciliation Officer
Advisory, Conciliation & Arbitration Service
Manchester

20 July 1990

Dear Sir

As per the negotiating and procedure agreement signed between the three Northern Minor Banks and the Building Society and Bank Workers Union a Joint Negotiating Meeting was held on 19 June 1990 in respect of pay in 1990. The following are details of pay claims submitted by BSBWU to be effective from 1 April 1990:

'1. "Across the board increase" in basic salaries of 12 per cent.
2. Large town allowance to be increased to £750.00.
3. Annual bonus to be increased to 8.33 per cent.

BSBWU also wishes to have joint negotiations under the procedure agreement with the three banks jointly.'

Accordingly, the negotiating and procedure agreement was signed covering three areas:

1. Annual basic salary negotiations.
2. Large town allowance.
3. Annual bonus.

At the above joint negotiating meeting, the banks made the following offer subject to the approval of the banks' head offices:

'1. *Across the board increase*: 8.1 per cent on salaries and salary scales from 1 April 1990.
2. *Annual bonus*: no increase in the current annual bonus rate of 3.5 per cent.
3. *Large town allowance*: it was agreed that discussion on these items would be deferred.'

The union rejected the banks' proposals on items 1. and 2. and registered a 'first failure to agree' under the terms of the procedural agreement.

A further meeting was held on the 2 July 1990 wherein BSBWU revised its claim as follows:

1. *Across the board increase*: 8.5 per cent on salary scale.
2. *Annual bonus*: 1.5 per cent increase on the current annual bonus rate of 3.5 per cent, i.e. annual bonus of 5 per cent.

The banks explained the justification for their earlier offer and again requested BSBWU to reconsider their proposal and accept what the banks have offered.

However, on rejection of the banks' request by BSBWU the banks have registered a 'second failure of agreement'.

We, therefore, in terms of an agreement with BSBWU, apply to yourselves for conciliation in the matter. The copy of the negotiating and procedure agreement is enclosed herewith for your information. If you need any other information, please contact the undersigned and also for organising the conciliation meeting.

Yours faithfully

R. Wilkinson

For: Chairman
       Joint Negotiating Committee Meeting
       Manchester

Encl. As above

Advisory, Conciliation and Arbitration Service

Mr R. Wilkinson
Lancashire Colliery Bank
Head Office
College Street
Bolton

24 July 1990

Dear Mr Wilkinson

Annual Pay Negotiations

I am writing to confirm that a meeting of the banks' Joint Negotiating Committee and BSBWU, under the auspices of ACAS, has been arranged for 10.30 a.m., 29 July 1990.

Yours sincerely

Arthur Riley
Senior Industrial Relations Officer

Advisory Conciliation and Arbitration Service

Refererence to arbitration

We hereby make application jointly for a difference between the under-mentioned parties to be referred to a single arbitrator, in the terms stated below:

Employer party:

Association of Northern Minor Banks

Employee party:

Building Society and Bank Workers Union

Terms of reference (defining the specific differences referred):

'To determine the appropriate increase in basic pay and annual bonus for local staff to be paid from 1 April 1990.'

Signed as authorised on behalf of the Employer party	Signed with the authority of my National Executive on behalf of the Employee Party

Status: Chairman JNC	Status: Negotiating Officer
Date: 29 July 1990	Date: 29 July 1990
	Note: This statement should be signed by a full time official of the union(s) concerned

Wilkes and Howarth Solicitors

St Mary's Walk
Manchester

13 August 1990

BSBWU
12 Cherry Street
Gorton
Manchester

Attention: H. Swales

Dear Sir

Northern Minor Banks

We have been instructed by the Lancashire Colliery Bank, the Cumbrian Woollen Bank and the Lancashire & Yorkshire Friendly Society Bank in connection with this year's pay negotiations. We understand that this year these three banks have been negotiating collectively and that there has been a failure to agree notwithstanding a meeting at ACAS.

We also understand that it is intended that there should be an arbitration although we are unclear as to the procedural position in that regard in the light of the terms of the procedural agreement. Perhaps you could let us know your understanding of the position.

There is one matter of great concern to us, however, and that is the question of bonus. Our clients inform us that the offer of 3.5 per cent bonus was made purely to maintain goodwill and to resolve the pay claim without protracted negotiation.

In the current situation, it is important therefore that, before any arbitration takes place, certain matters are clarified.

1. The terms of reference must be expressed so that the whole bonus issue is resolved once and for all. Our clients' position is that they accept negotiations for a proper profit or performance related scheme would be appropriate and they welcome your immediate comments on this. You will appreciate that at the moment there are no profits and therefore any such scheme might not be implemented for some time.
2. We need to know at once what is meant by 'bonus' in the current pay round. Do you mean enhanced pay, performance bonus, profit sharing, or what? Bonus cannot be paid in a complete vacuum and it seems to us this is not bonus at all but a lump sum across the board payment to enhance the pay award. Bonus means reward and is traditionally ex gratia. We await hearing from you urgently on this because these points need to be clarified before any arbitration proceeds.

We are copying this letter to ACAS as a matter of courtesy.

Yours faithfully

Wilkes and Howarth

Wilkes and Howarth Solicitors

St Mary's Walk
Manchester

27 August 1990

BSBWU
12 Cherry Street
Gorton
Manchester

Attention: H. Swales

Dear Sir

Northern Minor Banks

We refer to our letter of 13 August and are disappointed not to have had a reply. We appreciate you spoke with Mr Hartley of this office on 19 August, but you will appreciate we cannot proceed with this arbitration without the points referred to in our letter being clarified.

It matters not that there has been an agreed reference to arbitration. The difficulty is caused by the use of the undefined term 'bonus'. Having attended last year's arbitration you will appreciate that it would be quite wrong to go into this year's arbitration without, at the very least, revised terms of reference in relation to bonus. May we please, therefore, hear from you as a matter of urgency with a full and detailed response to the two points in the second page of our letter. You will appreciate we cannot advise our clients to proceed with the arbitration until these points are clarified in writing.

Yours faithfully,

Wilkes and Howarth

The Building Society and Bank Workers Union

12 Cherry Street
Gorton
Manchester

27 August 1990

Wilkes and Howarth Solicitors
St Mary's Walk
Manchester

Dear Sirs

Northern Minor Banks

I was somewhat surprised to receive your letter of 27 August 1990 relating to the definition of bonus.

As stated in our telephone conversation, we regard bonus simply as being a sum of money paid over and above basic salary. This payment may be made for a variety of reasons.

I look forward to confirmation of the arrangements for 9 September 1990 and assume that in accordance with normal practice we shall exchange cases seven days beforehand.

Yours sincerely

Harold Swales
Chief Negotiating Officer

Wilkes and Howarth Solicitors

St Mary's Walk
Manchester

1 September 1990

BSBWU
12 Cherry Street
Gorton
Manchester

Attention: H. Swales

Dear Sirs

Northern Minor Banks

We thank you for your letter of 27 August. We must make it plain that we are advising our clients they should not proceed with this arbitration until such time as the position in relation to bonus is clarified. In the light of the arbitration decision last year, we do not think it is appropriate to go into this year's arbitration without some further definition of what you are seeking in regard to bonus. As presently stated, it seems as though you are simply asking for what is, in effect, increased wages.

It must be understood that this is wholly unacceptable. A bonus can be paid, as you point out, for a variety of reasons, but we would submit all of those reasons are in some way related to merit or effort, or possibly the results of merit or effort. Simply to pay a lump sum over and above a wage settlement and call it bonus is, in our view, unacceptable and certainly not what was anticipated by last year's arbitration panel.

We are prepared to advise our clients to go into arbitration if bonus is to be characterised properly as a reward for effort or, let us say, enhanced profitability. You will readily appreciate that, in circumstances where our clients are making losses, this point is very material. Our clients are simply not prepared to pay an extra sum over and above a proper level of wage award and call it bonus simply because this has been done in the past.

Yours faithfully

Wilkes and Howarth

The Building Society and Bank Workers Union

12 Cherry Street
Gorton
Manchester

2 September 1990

Mr R. Pollard
Cumbrian Woollen Bank
Castle Square
Carlisle

Dear Mr Pollard

I have received from Messrs Wilkes and Howarth a letter stating that they are advising the banks not to proceed with the arbitration 'until such time as the position in relation to bonus is clarified'.

As you are well aware, this is partly the purpose of the hearing and we regard this move as being provocative in the extreme.

The banks have had a year to suggest some kind of performance related bonus, but have made no effort to do so.

Please be advised that unless I receive confirmation that the arbitration hearing will go ahead as scheduled on 9 September, the union will hold the banks in breach of procedure and commence balloting for industrial action.

Yours sincerely

Harold Swales
Chief Negotiating Officer

Wilkes and Howarth Solicitors

St Mary's Walk
Manchester

5 September 1990

BSBWU
12 Cherry Street
Gorton
Manchester

Dear Sirs

We are writing in reply to your letter to our clients of 2 September which has been overtaken by events, in that by reason of the unavailability of the arbitrator, the arbitration will not in any event be taking place on 9 October.

Our clients are prepared to proceed to arbitration in accordance with the agreed procedures. However, as you know the subject of a 'bonus' payment was considered at length in last year's arbitration for the Cumbrian Woollen Bank. The unanimous recommendation of the arbitrators was that a bonus scheme should be negotiated which was performance related at least to some degree. This is of course the very nature of bonus, which is a reward for merit. There is a fundamental distinction between this, and what the union is currently seeking, which is a further 5 per cent pay rise in addition to the basic review, and as such this claim is arguably outside the scope of reference for the arbitration.

We will, therefore, be writing to the arbitrator requesting that this issue is resolved either by a hearing prior to the main arbitration hearing or as a preliminary point at the arbitration hearing itself.

May we please ask you to correspond through us.

Yours faithfully

Wilkes and Howarth

The Building Society and Bank Workers Union

12 Cherry Street
Gorton
Manchester

9 September 1990

Mr R. Pollard
Cumbrian Woollen Bank
Castle Square
Carlisle

Dear Mr Pollard

re: Forthcoming arbitration

I am in receipt of a letter dated 5 September 1990 from Messrs Wilkes and Howarth concerning the forthcoming arbitration.

Obviously, I am fully aware of the award made last year concerning the nature of the bonus payment. As you are aware, we made clear both during negotiations and at ACAS that as the banks have failed to come forward with a performance related scheme, that we would pursue our original claim.

At this late stage, I must advise you that under no circumstances whatsoever are we prepared to re-negotiate the terms of reference agreed at ACAS and neither will we be prepared to have any kind of preliminary hearing relating to the bonus.

Messrs Wilkes and Howarth have asked that we correspond directly with them, but we are not prepared to do this as they are not party to the procedural agreement. I repeat my confirmation that we are prepared and ready to attend an arbitration on 30 September and trust that this causes no problems to the banks.

Yours sincerely

Harold Swales
Chief Negotiating Officer

Wilkes and Howarth Solicitors

St Mary's Walk
Manchester

16 September 1990
Arbitrator
Northern Minor Banks
ACAS
Manchester

Dear Sir

Pay Review 1990 – Northern Minor Banks

We have recently been instructed on behalf of the Northern Minor Banks in connection with the 1990 pay arbitration with BSBWU. We understand that this is to be heard on the morning of 30 September.

From the associated documents, you will see that, on our advice, our clients have taken issue with the union over the terms of reference to arbitration, with respect to 'bonus'. In view of the confusion over the nature of the bonus payment at last year's arbitration we are of the opinion that it is essential to clarify at this stage, the terms of reference for 'bonus'. Last year's arbitration award for the banks stated that in view of the uncertainties regarding the bonus scheme, the arbitrator recommended that the parties negotiate a revised bonus scheme which should be performance related to at least some degree. No negotiations have taken place, although when an approach about this was made to BSBWU the response was that it was up to the banks to propose such a scheme.

We will therefore be asking that the arbitrator clarifies the terms of reference in relation to bonus. It is our clear view that a bonus scheme must be profit or performance related, rather than simply an across the board supplement to a pay award which is how BSBWU sees it.

Perhaps this point could be taken first at the hearing and only after it has been resolved would questions of pay awards be considered.

Yours faithfully

Wilkes and Howarth

Questions

1 Is a bonus a worker's right or a management prerogative?
2 Should the Northern Minor Banks be expected to match the salary scales of the major national banks?
3 Do you think that the calling in of solicitors by the banks was a helpful move or not?

GLOSSARY

ACAS Advisory, Conciliation and Arbitration Service

ADR Alternative Dispute Resolution

Advisee person who is advised

Advisory first stage of the process leading to arbitration once a dispute has been referred to ACAS

Agreement a set of procedures mutually agreed between the Trades Unions and the employer which cover most aspects of work

Arbitration the resolution of a dispute by reference to an unbiased and independent person or panel

Arbitrator an unbiased and independent person who decides upon a dispute referred to them

Associated documents additional material to the employer's case and the union case which is accepted as fact by both sides (e.g. Codes of Practice, Joint Agreements) or correspondence of which both sides are aware

Basic pay standard pay rates or salary before overtime or bonuses are added

Bonus payment extra to basic pay given on the basis of individual performance (e.g. productivity) or by the employer across the organisation (e.g. related to company profit)

Conciliation the process of trying to reach an agreement between the two parties by an official of ACAS

Demarcation the boundary of work practice which shall be conducted by members of one profession or union compared with another

Dismissal termination of employment

Dispute a grievance raised to a formal level between management and union

Failure to agree formal indication of the collapse of negotiations between management and union

Grievance a complaint by a worker, or group of workers against the employer, usually with the support of the union

Industrial relations the relationship between employer and employees over all aspects of the world of work

IPR Individual Performance Review

IRS Inland Revenue Service

Job evaluation a process of comparing one job with another

Job grading a process of placing jobs in bands or groups

JNC Joint Negotiating Committees

Leading hand the leader of a very small group of people usually operating one machine or controlling a process

Lock-out term given to an employer's unilateral closure of a factory or business for reasons other than lack of orders or lack of money

Pay parity the quest for pay equal to a standard rate or equal to that of another group of workers

Pay scale pay rates set out according to job grades or other means of differentiating between workers

Procedure set of actions to be followed in the event of particular occurrences, e.g. grievance procedure, disciplinary procedure

PRP Performance Related Pay

Reward means of rewarding employees, usually other than basic pay

Submission union or employer's case to the Arbitrator

Supervisor person in charge of a group of workers and who allocates their work

Terms of Reference the statement of the dispute and the boundaries of the solution agreed by both sides for the Arbitrator to determine

TUC Trades Union Congress, the overall policy-making body to which most unions belong

Unfair dismissal wrongful termination of employment

Union body set up to safeguard the interests of particular groups of workers, usually Trades Union

Wage drift the increase in payments over time due to bonus, overtime or annual increment payments in addition to normal wage rate increases